FROM FRANCHISE TO LOCAL DIVE

MULTIPLYING YOUR CHURCH BY DISCOVERING YOUR CONTEXTUAL FLAVOR

JASON MOORE & ROSARIO PICARDO

Foreword by Paul Nixon

From Franchise to Local Dive

Multiplying Your Church by Discovering Your Contextual Flavor

books@marketsquarebooks.com
P.O. Box 23664 Knoxville, Tennessee 37933

ISBN: 978-1-950899-09-8
Library of Congress: 2020933778

Printed and Bound in the United States of America

Publisher: Kevin Slimp
Editor: Kristin Lighter
Post-Process Editor: Ken Rochelle
Graphics and Cover: Jason Moore

Scripture quotations noted as follows:

NLT

NIV

MSG

ESV

Roz and Jason would like to thank:

A book like this does not happen without supportive family, friends, and colleagues. We'd like to thank Erin Mackenzie and Wesley Palmer for their help editing this book, even before it went to the editors. We appreciate you helping us make *Franchise to Local Dive* better.

Paul Nixon: You've been a planting guru and superstar for many years and we continually look up to you. Thanks for writing our foreword, and for setting the tone of the book right from the start.

We are very grateful to the many pastors, planters, friends and revitalizers who agreed to be interviewed for this book. We had even more on our list than we had time to interview. Thanks Jorge Acevedo, Jacob Armstrong, Chris Aytes, Scott Chrostek, Rachel Gilmore, Sara Heath, Yvette Massey, Emily McGinley, Matt Miofsky, Stacy Piyakhun, Brent Ross and Adam Weber for allowing us to speak with you and tell your stories. Your vulnerability with our readers moves this work to the next level.

Jason would like to thank:

There's no way I could have written this book, or done many of the things I've accomplished in the last couple of decades, without the support of my wife and soulmate, Michele. She is my partner in all things, and I'm thankful for her support in this too. I love you more than I can express in words.

Roz, I love you like a brother. I'm so glad our paths crossed and our stories have become shared in so many ways. Thanks for your patience when the busyness of my schedule put us far behind the curve.

Thanks also to Kevin Slimp at Market Square Books for sticking with us all this time. You are a courageous entrepreneur, and it's awesome to see you having such great success.

Blair Zant, thank you for your honesty in sharing some critical feedback that made this book what it needed to be – a more complete picture of who the church is.

I'd like to thank our many friends and supporters who have made my ministry possible these last 20+ years. Thanks to those who have hosted my seminars, hired me as a consultant, commissioned me to create art/media and encouraged me to do what I do. I am blessed beyond measure by your support, and I don't take the role you've played in my life for granted.

I'd like to dedicate my portion of this book to my son Ethan Robert – quite the prolific writer and artist himself – and to my daughter Madeline Darby who is a creative and artistic soul in her own right. I love you both, and look forward to watching you accomplish your wildest dreams.

Roz would like to thank:

I want to thank my wonderful wife, Callie Picardo, our two children – Lily and Gabriella – and soon to born, Hannah. I appreciate the willingness and help of my church, Mosaic, and my co-pastor Wayne Botkin. I also want to thank the excellent staff and faculty of United Theological Seminary and Rev. Dr. Kent Millard.

Table of Contents

Foreword 1
by Paul Nixon

Introduction 5

Chapter One 27
Franchise: Established Churches

Chapter Two 49
The Local Drive: Organic Communities

Chapter Three 85
Menu Planning: The Covenant Agreement

Chapter Four 107
Eat Fresh: New Possibilities

Chapter Five 127
Discovering Your Local Flavor: Incarnational Ministry

Chapter Six 155
Team Cuisine: Fostering Collaboration

Chapter Seven 183
Worth the Wait: Essential Ingredients

Chapter Eight 233
To Go Box: Next Steps

A few years ago, a friend and I began collecting models of faith communities that are thriving in the western world. Our list grew long; there are so many great ways that people do church all around us, ways that thrive easily and engage plenty of people. In thriving churches, just as in thriving restaurants, the room fills up at prime hours, and sometimes a line snakes down the sidewalk as people wait their turn to get in!

The vast array of thriving ministry stories surprised us, since we see so many churches in their late-life cycle and decline. Then we realized that almost all of the failing churches fall into one category. They are franchise-mentality operations who derive their core identity, best ideas, curriculum, branding logo, and possibly even their communion wafers from a denominational headquarters and warehouse somewhere.

And the result can be summed up in a word (or a snore): *zzzzzzz*. Franchise-based church is truly an endangered species in many places.

Mind you, there are some savvy franchises in today's retail world. They pop up fast and spread across the land with nimble practices and excellent customer awareness, complete with a downloadable app that makes ordering easy. I cannot think of one Christian denomination that operates like this. The innovations that drive most denominations happened generations ago. If the average person were to walk into almost any denominationally oriented church in their community, they would be simply baffled by the whole experience. Hey, our kids grew up in these places and they are baffled. Why do we expect a different reaction from the neighbors? A lot of folks experience extreme disconnect between pre-packaged church and the local context of their lives.

But some churches are different. They may be denominationally affiliated or not. Either way, they understand that they are one-of-a-kind, on a unique journey with God. Their gifts, their context, and their journey are unlike any other church in the world. And they build their ministry from that understanding. You go to their website or their worship service and you immediately realize this place is all about fresh cooking!

One of the churches that I call home recently went through a visioning season, from which they added a core value that will soon appear on their website. I was not involved in the meetings. I was simply attending worship the day they reported back to us. (Core values describe *how we roll* as a local church, in all that we do, and every time we gather.) The newly stated core value at our church is *play*. Our pastor is a former stand-up comic. Our church artfully and appropriately mixes laughter with even the most serious of gatherings. I can't imagine us gathering without intentional playfulness woven into things. Playfulness is how we roll. It's a part of the way we are called to live out the Gospel, and the fact that this church boldly lives into its uniqueness is directly related to the fact that we have to arrive early to get a decent seat!

Some of the most vibrant churches in North America are multi-site and sometimes there is a strong franchise vibe from one location to the next. In these cases, the components being franchised are relatively recent and relatively local. If the mother campus is overflowing with people serving up a certain kind of spiritual menu, the chances are good that they will be able to draw a crowd a few miles down the road with a similar menu. This kind of franchising is quite different than basing our ministry decisions on institutional strategies that developed far from our zip code, and possibly far from the time in which we find ourselves. Yet, even in this case, most multi-site churches still make allowance for contextual differences from one ministry site to the next because neighborhoods can vary wildly.*

In this delightful book, *Franchise to Local Dive*, Jason and Roz help us think through what it means to live into the local story that God is seeking to write through our lives in the places we gather as church! As always, there will be a common gospel foundation that changes little from age to age or from one place to the next. But the ways that the core ingredients might come together – the possibilities are staggering! And, honestly, a big part of the fun is to find ourselves in the kitchen as God cooks up something fresh, something so lovely that it may well cause our neighbors to line up down the street to get in!

---

* For more on how most multi-site churches customize ministry from one location to the next, see my book *Multi: The Chemistry of Church Diversity*, The Pilgrim Press, 2019.

People have no problem waiting in line if the food is really good. Years ago, I found myself on a sidewalk, waiting for twenty minutes to get into St. John's United Methodist in Houston, where Rudy and Juanita Rasmus are pastors. As I waited, I visited with the woman next to me in line. I discovered that this was her first Sunday out of prison, and that she and her young daughter were going to church together for the very first time. She was so excited. Little did I know that she would make her public profession of faith about ninety minutes later inside the sanctuary. I asked her why she had chosen St. John's on her first Sunday out of prison. She said it was simple: they had visited her and loved her inside the prison walls. This should remind us that even when there's great food served inside our sanctuaries, it's best to begin by giving people a taste out in the varied places we find them.

I hope you and your leaders are energized by this read as you get into the kitchen with God to prepare something profoundly local and fresh!

Paul Nixon

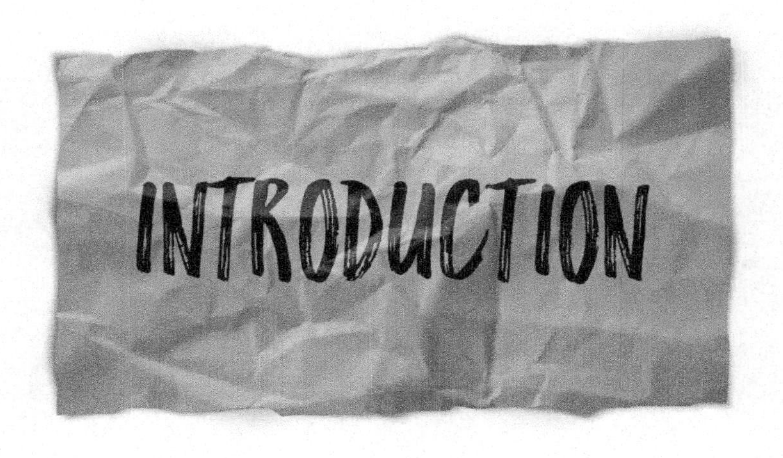
INTRODUCTION

When you're in the mood to go out for a great meal, where's your favorite place to go? In the town where you live, where are the most popular places to dine? The hottest places in town likely have a great reputation, an appealing ambiance, and food worth waiting in long lines for.

Whether it's a nationally known franchise or a hidden gem of a local dive, the best places draw crowds from near and far. They seem to have the pull to draw a nearly unstoppable customer base indefinitely to their locations. But even the most popular of eateries can find themselves shuttered after years, or even decades, of successful operation.

Drive through just about any city and you're likely to pass at least one boarded-up restaurant with a "Space Available - For Rent" sign somewhere on the building. No matter how vibrant a place once was, or how many four-star reviews it once boasted, for any number of reasons, the tastes of the customer base shifted to the point of unsustainability.

The story is the same in the church. Many local churches are stuck in a rut, have reached a plateau or, worst of all, are declining. The temptation churches often face is to serve up the exact same ministry models that have worked in another time and space. These models feel comfortable and safe. The problem, however, is that they have become stale, predictable, processed, and formulaic. They may have worked for a specific church community with specific resources, or maybe they were rooted in charismatic leadership. Yet, like serving items from the menu at a franchise restaurant and expecting the food to be palatable in the local context, many churches fail to discover what their local community is actually hungry for.

The transition from franchise to local is all about cooking with the local flavor that will resonate in a given community. Rather than attempting to franchise, inserting the proven recipe of an established church and brand into a community, churches would see better results and would better serve their communities by infusing local flavor into every aspect of their ministries. With a focus on freshness, quality, and innovation, churches can thrive, grow, and create powerful movements.

From Franchise to Local Dive explores what it means for churches to cook with local flavor. What does mass-production miss when it comes to church, and what can we learn from our culture's current obsession with local dives? Local dives give up economies of scale, but the advantages more than make up for the loss. What chains offer in consistency, they lack in creativity, contextualization, and authenticity. The local church is not called to settle as a chain fast food restaurant that cranks out disciples. Rather, the call is to be a local, homegrown, farm-fresh, organic ministry using the best available ingredients.

This book is intended for church leaders, clergy, lay people, and congregations who are struggling to stay or become relevant in their surrounding communities. So many churches find themselves in a rut, cooking up the same old recipes while expecting different results. Or, they try to throw in a few new spices they've picked up at a seminar or read from a step-by-step book like this one. These churches often look to a nearby megachurch and hope that emulating that church's practices in their own communities will produce the same results the megachurch has experienced. Instead, by ignoring their local context, these congregations end up with dated, sterile, and predictable ministry practices. Our hope is that leaders and churches find their own voice and transform their churches in a way that a franchise approach will not achieve. While churches can and should look to each other for best practices, we will also encourage churches to seek implementation from their own contexts.

The intent of this book is not to give you a new recipe. It's not meant to suggest a pinch of this, a dash of that, and "Ta-da! Bon appétit!" - there's your local dive. We can't supply you with your recipe. But we will help you explore how to discover your local flavor, share some stories of how others have learned to make the leap to becoming a local dive, and teach you some basics about what makes a good recipe.

We hope you will be challenged to tap into your community's local ingredients and appetites. How do you connect with what the community has to offer? What are they hungry for? The answers to these questions will affect everything from branding to worship to discipleship. It will define the metaphors we use and the stories we tell. Jason and Roz bring different, but equally valuable, experiences to this topic.

Jason and Roz met in 2013 at a conference of pastors and laypeople in New England, where they were each slated to give keynote addresses. The two hit it off, and Jason (a former staff person at Ginghamsburg UMC) mentioned to Roz that Ginghamsburg was looking for a director of new church development. Several weeks later, Roz joined the team. Roz and Jason have become close friends, and their collaboration on this project is a labor of love and friendship.

For the past two decades, Jason Moore has been a regular speaker, workshop leader, and keynoter at local, regional, and international events across North America. In the last five years, his speaking engagements have increased from fifteen or twenty annually to over thirty events per year. Jason is also a nationally known author, worship coach, and concept/media designer. His role as the first graphic designer/original worship design team member at Ginghamsburg UMC provided his initial platform. He has been hired by twelve United Methodist Annual Conferences to lead the process of designing worship, media, theming, and other creative aspects of the yearly annual conference experience. In 2016, he was hired to design the media for and collaborate with Bishop Gregory Palmer on the United Methodist General Conference Episcopal address.

Rosario "Roz" Picardo is an up-and-coming church leader whose influence continues to grow. Known for his pioneering work of resuscitating dying congregations and planting new ones, Rosario has become a sought-after speaker and coach. His specialties are leadership and new faith community development. Roz has served small, medium, and large churches in urban and suburban areas. As founding and lead pastor of Mosaic Church and former Executive Pastor of New Church Development at Ginghamsburg UMC, Roz has the experience and track record from which to launch this new title.

This project was inspired in part by the popular television show *Diners, Drive-Ins and Dives*. For those not familiar with the show, host Guy Fieri travels off the beaten path to roadside diners, vintage drive-ins, and out-of-the-way dives, enjoying some of the best-kept secrets of greasy-spoon eateries across America. You'll never see Guy visit an Applebee's, Red Lobster, or KFC. He visits establishments viewers may have never heard of, but that tend to be well-known in their own regions. These restaurants may not rapidly mass-produce their food, be listed on the New York Stock Exchange, or boast multi-million-dollar profits from operating in multiple locations, but their flavor speaks for itself. It's truly one-of-a kind fare, and people love it. There's nothing about it that is stale, sterile, or processed. Instead, it's satisfying with homegrown taste.

There's something really special about a local dive. People will drive miles—cruising past the exits boasting convenient franchises—to experience it. This seasoning and flavor is not only a recipe for a great meal, but it can teach us something about our own attempts to make disciples by sharing the

Word of God in a homegrown, local way. A big-box, one-size-fits-all approach deprives churches and their communities of the unique tastes that have developed through the years because of a region's history, climate, agriculture, and people.

The movement toward eating local has exploded in recent years, but there is nothing new under the sun. We see churches have attempted once again to be incarnational in their communities. The days of "If you build it, they will come" are over. Going out to the people and understanding the community is essential for ministry vitality. The only way to discover the local flavor is to get out of the office.

We take our biblical foundation for this book from Nehemiah 8, where Ezra reads the law to the people. As he does this, the Levites cooked with local ingredients by translating the law into the language of the people. Prior to this translation, the people had no access to the law. They couldn't afford to patronize the franchise, but they stood for six hours listening to the local version.

This is exactly what we see served up to the people of God in Ezra's day as the people rediscovered what it meant to eat well in Nehemiah 8:1-4a, 6, and 8-12 (ESV). The franchise of the day was written law in the temple, accessible only to a select few. Ezra decides to take the scriptures out to the people.

> [1] *all the people gathered together into the square before the Water Gate. They told the scribe Ezra to bring the book of the law of Moses, which the Lord had given to Israel.* [2] *Accordingly, the priest Ezra brought the law before the assembly, both men and women and all who could hear with understanding. This was on the first day of the seventh month.* [3] *He read from it facing the square before the Water Gate from early morning until midday, in the presence of the men and the women and those who could understand; and the ears of all the*

people were attentive to the book of the law. [4] The scribe Ezra stood on a wooden platform that had been made for the purpose.

[6] Then Ezra blessed the Lord, the great God, and all the people answered, "Amen, Amen," lifting up their hands. Then they bowed their heads and worshiped the Lord with their faces to the ground.

[8] So they read from the book, from the law of God, with interpretation. They gave the sense, so that the people understood the reading.

[9] And Nehemiah, who was the governor, and Ezra the priest and scribe, and the Levites who taught the people said to all the people, "This day is holy to the Lord your God; do not mourn or weep." For all the people wept when they heard the words of the law.

[10] Then he said to them, "Go your way, eat the fat and drink sweet wine and send portions of them to those for whom nothing is prepared, for this day is holy to our Lord; and do not be grieved, for the joy of the Lord is your strength."

[11] So the Levites stilled all the people, saying, "Be quiet, for this day is holy; do not be grieved." [12] And all the people went their way to eat and drink and to send portions and to make great rejoicing, because they had understood the words that were declared to them.

One of Roz's favorite books of the Bible is Nehemiah. Nehemiah isn't a prophet, but he hears from God. Nehemiah isn't a priest, but he is known for his walk with God. Nehemiah isn't a king, but he hangs with royalty. Nehemiah is a cup-bearer whose job it was to protect the king at all costs. At the end of Nehemiah's prayer in chapter 1:11 he says, "At the time, I was cup-bearer to the king." Nehemiah's role was simple; he had to sample the king's wine before the king drank out of the cup. (If you are a wine connoisseur, this would have been the job for you!) Just one catch: if the wine were poisoned, well, you know the rest. Nehemiah faced some on-the-job hazards.

As a holy man seeking after God and wanting to see his people protected, Nehemiah sees Jerusalem in ruins and knows something has to be done. Without fortified walls, Jerusalem was susceptible to attacks, and the people were left in unrest. Nehemiah prays and fasts before the Lord for days. He goes from being cup-bearer to the king to strategic leader. Nehemiah first approaches King Xerxes to voice his concern. The king is so moved he decides to bankroll the project to fortify the city. Later in the story, we read that each household helped build a portion of the wall, despite naysayers and persecutors. The wall is rebuilt in a miraculous fifty-two days. However, spiritual revival doesn't break out simply because of a building project or because of one epic leader's vision. It happens through people gathered together as one. It's not Nehemiah on the main stage serving up the meal for the people, but Ezra the scribe.

The reason for this is found in verse 1:

All the people gathered together into the square before the Water Gate. They told the scribe Ezra to bring the book of the law of Moses, which the Lord had given to Israel.

Now the people that gathered that day in Jerusalem were part of the 42,000 returnees from Persia.[1]

Nehemiah 8:1

---

[1] Carter, Charles E. *The Emergence of Yehud in the Persian Period: A Social and Demographic Study* (Sheffield, UK: Sheffield Academic Press, 1999), 297.

Their situation was not too different from that of the Hebrew slaves returning from Egypt, as they too had been in captivity and were forced to live in a foreign culture, speak a different language, and observe the culture customs of their society.

Ezra reads from the law for six or seven hours, according to Neh. 8:3.[2] Ezra stands on a huge platform and addresses the crowd. Remember, we are talking about 50,000 people! This shows that people will wait a long time for the best meal served up right.

Think of your favorite restaurant. For the best meal, you are willing to wait in line even if you have a reservation. It's the quality of the food, perhaps the service, or the ambiance that contributes to the dining experience. On the other hand, people get frustrated waiting in a long line at a drive-thru because they are expecting *fast* food. They know they are accepting sub-par quality and extra calories for speed and convenience.

Just as people are today, the people in Nehemiah 8 were hungry for God. They were willing to stand for six hours listening to Ezra preach. They knew the stories. They knew their parents and grandparents had been exiled because they disobeyed the Law of God. They knew from the brokenness of those stories, they knew from the brokenness of their walls, and the brokenness of their own lives, that they needed God. This was a meal worth waiting for.

This seems impossible today, right? Can you imagine sitting in one spot and listening to one person speak or read for six hours straight on any topic? Even though it seems that our society increasingly wants nothing to do with God,

---

[2] Throntveit, Mark A. "Application: Sermon-Prayer of Confession." *Ezra-Nehemiah*, (Louisville, KY: Westminster John Knox Press, 2012), 102.

we believe we are seeing a generation that is increasingly hungry for God. People are tired of the mass-produced, big-box franchise, "perfected" recipe. And, fortunately, our God meets us where we are to sit and have a meal with us. As society becomes more broken and individual lives experience more brokenness, the watered-down, flavorless, sugary way we do church no longer whets people's appetites. We all want something of substance, something filling and life-giving.

Franchises are recognizing that people want something less "cookie cutter" and processed. McDonald's recently re-conceptualized the Quarter Pounder, boasting "fresh—not frozen" beef. What a novel concept! They had no choice but to fall in line when competing chains like Smashburger and Five Guys Burgers began with that practice from the start. The desire for something more real is upon us, both in the food industry and the church. Maybe we're collectively asking, as Wendy's once did, "Where's the beef?"

Ezra brought the meal to the people, and it was flavored to their liking. They could actually understand the Word when it was spoken. It was palatable and right in front of them. At a time in America when the economy is shaky (yet even modest big-city restaurant spaces involve multi-million-dollar build-outs), when consumers have wearied of giant chains but still crave food that is novel, inexpensive, and fast, food trucks are the new incubators of innovation.

They are nimble, have low overhead, and can move to where their recipes are most desirable. Menu not connecting? Change it up! Experimentation is easy in this scenario. No lines formed outside the window? Move the truck to a new location.

In Dayton, Ohio where Roz and Jason live, there is a beloved local dive called Zombie Dogz. Zombie Dogz began in 2012 as a food truck serving up amazing hot dogs with zombie themes like The Nibbler, Sliced and Diced, and The Walking Dead.[3]

As the owners traveled from food truck rallies to fairs and other gatherings, they would experiment and perfect their creations. These trailblazers were awarded "Best Food Truck in Ohio" in *Ohio Magazine*'s Best of Ohio Readers' Ballot.[4]

ZOMBIE DOGZ FOOD TRUCK

In a short five years, their customers had become so loyal, they began to think of them as friends and family. Customers would literally follow the truck wherever it went to enjoy their favorite dog.

Demand grew to the point where the next logical step was to open a brick and mortar store near the University of Dayton. Some customers mourned the end of the food truck, and their outcries were heard. The food truck made a comeback a few years later.[5] Even in the midst of their transition, Zombie Dogz maintained the ethos of what began with their mobile restaurant on wheels.[6] However, because of the

3 "Zombie Dogz Dayton Menu." Zombie Dogz Dayton Ohio Gourmet Dogs, www.zombiedogzdayton.com/menu. Accessed December 4, 2019.

4 Fisher, Mark. "Local Food Truck Pioneer Zombie Dogz to Park the Truck for Good." *Dayton Daily News*, October 28, 2017, www.daytondailynews.com/news/local/local-food-truck-pioneer-zombie-dogz-park-the-truck-for-good/Ee5fYL-FOlLmjlpQMoWdENN/.

5 Fisher, Mark. "Local Food Truck Rises from the Dead." *Dayton Daily News,* (22 June, 2018), www.daytondailynews.com/places/restaurant/deep-fried-zombie-balls-come-flavors-you-can-taste-them-this-weekend-only/Lm7TX7xX6qKVdntVmtinVK/.

6 Ibid.

popularity of the food truck and an outcry of its supporters, their website states their commitment like this:

"Zombie Dogz offers its patrons a convenient, economical, and exciting alternative to the everyday, mundane fast food chains. ZD strives to provide a growing list of gourmet hot dog combinations along with handcrafted side dishes, using farm fresh and locally made foods. Mission Statement and seasonality: To consistently provide our valued guests with impeccable service by demonstrating friendliness, graciousness, efficiency, knowledge, professionalism, and integrity in our work. To create and maintain a business that is comprehensive and exceptional in its attention to every detail of operation. To develop lasting relationships with customers, creating a niche following. To keep our concept fresh, stimulating and on the cutting edge of the food service industry."[7]

Food trucks are an example of a recession creating innovation. North America is still climbing out of recession, and it's not just a financial recession. We're facing spiritual poverty as well. To make matters worse, the church itself has become bankrupt. For the past fifty years, we have built our churches to serve commuters with the mentality that if we simply build it, people will come and feed themselves. We got good at drawing in commuters instead of building communities. The food we have served has lost its flavor because we stopped experimenting in the kitchen. We cook with the same ingredients from recipes that originated elsewhere, rather than appealing to the people in our own neighborhoods. When we look around, we see that our communities have changed. Our church buildings have become museums instead of missional outposts, no longer serving their original purposes.

---

[7] "Zombie Dogz Dayton Menu." *Zombie Dogz Dayton Ohio Gourmet Dogs*, www.zombiedogzdayton.com/menu. Accessed 12/4/19.

We can either close the kitchens, or we can create a new menu, jump in a truck, and take it to the people.

One church has made their name in Houston, Texas, without any space of their own. But they do have an actual food truck. St. Isidore Episcopal Church was planted in 2015 as a new faith community. When Houston was flooded in 2017 by Hurricane Harvey, this small new church went out to meet the needs of their community through food. They have served thousands of meals since Hurricane Harvey with their full-time food truck ministry. In the words of parishioner Molly Carr, St. Isidore "is really about community, about building relationship around the table."[8] The church also meets in a variety of locations around Houston—in bars, restaurants, apartment complexes, and laundromats. It's a church without walls, on the move, going out to where the people are.[9]

ABUNDANT HARVEST FOOD TRUCK, SPRING, TX

What are the people in your community hungry for? If you aren't going to the people with your food truck and asking

[8] Paulsen, David. "Food Truck Ministry Creates Sacred Space Outside Church." *The Christian Century*, www.christiancentury.org/article/news/food-truck-ministry-creates-sacred-space-outside-church. December 17, 2017.

[9] Ibid.

them, you will never know. What Ezra did was provide a meal that the people hadn't tasted before in the local flavor that was easy to digest. Once they tasted it, they couldn't get enough. The people truly experienced Psalm 34:18: "Taste and see that the Lord is good!"

How do we know that they enjoyed the meal and couldn't get enough?

Everyone continues to stand on their feet. Ezra then praises God in Neh. 8:6. "God you are great! You have been so good to us!" And everyone—imagine 50,000 voices—saying, "AMEN!" which means, "So be it! Lord, we see the Scriptures as your Word. What you say is true. What you say about yourself is true. We agree with it all!" This shows us that they were not worshiping the book, but the God who wrote it.

The meal was seasoned and presented to the people in a way that made the difference, in a local flavor. Verse 8 says, "They read from the Book of the Law of God and clearly explained the meaning of what was being read, helping the people understand each passage" (Nehemiah, 8:8, NLT). Small group leaders were interacting with them, explaining the Scripture to them, and answering their questions. Notice the words, "making it clear," or "translating it." They helped people understand the text. Many in the crowd were from Persia and perhaps did not know much of the Hebrew language. Most were likely biblically illiterate as well.

Ezra is teaching us that disciples aren't made in a franchise model. As pastors, we have become so focused on denominational and ecclesiastical pressures to mass produce and increase numbers by impressing the crowds, that we have opted to serve fast food instead of something unique, different, and with a local flavor. Local flavor means using real ingredients.

One night Roz was on his way to church to attend a meeting. With his belly growling at him, he stopped for a bite to eat. You may be familiar with the restaurant he chose: it's a local Irish joint called McDonald's. Yes, they're fast and you know what you're going to get there. But let's take a look at the list of ingredients in some of this food. It may frighten you. Much of the ground beef in fast food is treated with the ammonia by-product that Jamie Oliver calls "pink slime." Oliver highlights some of the other ingredients McDonald's uses:

1. **Propylene glycol:** A substance similar to that found in antifreeze. *The International Business Times* calls this additive the "less toxic" version of ethylene glycol, which is a dangerous anti-freeze.
2. **Ammonium sulfate**: Used to encourage dough to rise in fast food buns. The chemical composition of this additive is akin to the wash for meat trimmings.
3. **Azodicarbonamide**: An odorless synthetic chemical mostly used in the production of foamed plastics.
4. **Sodium acid pyrophosphate:** A buffering agent, used for both food and industrial purposes. Its function: Maintain color, improve water holding capacity, maintain stability during heating and other functions. Found in chicken nuggets.
5. **Calcium silicate:** The white powder is often used to prevent bricks, roof tiles, and cement from caking. It is found in Angus beef patty and seasonings.[10]

---

[10] MBD, "Hamburger Chef Jamie Oliver Proves McDonald's Burgers 'Unfit for Human Consumption.'" *Political Blind Spot.* www.politicalblindspot.com/hamburger-chef-jamie-oliver-proves-mcdonalds-burgers-unfit-for-human-consumption/. August 23, 2014.

This doesn't sound appetizing, yet millions of Americans put it into their bodies every day. It's not healthy, and the effects of processed food can take a toll on the body.

If you don't believe us, just watch the documentary *Super Size Me* where the director, star, and participant Morgan Spurlock almost died from eating nothing but McDonald's for thirty days straight, while gaining twenty-four pounds and suffering health complications like heart palpitations.[11]

When the church doesn't change its menu and serves up its version of fast food, it creates disciples who are lethargic and possibly spiritually unhealthy. A one-size-fits-all approach doesn't work.

Now you may be thinking, *Roz and Jason, you have worked for one of the best-known franchises in Methodism. Who are you to dis the franchise?* We can understand that question, and you're not wrong to ask it.

However, at the core of the work we've done as planters/ coaches and developers of new faith communities is intentionality. It's not easy to think local dive when the franchise has had such an incredible run. It takes a delicate balance. The oldest campus of Ginghamsburg Church, Tipp City, was actually founded in 1863. But God used pioneer Mike Slaughter, who didn't arrive until 1979. The church started to experience growth as Slaughter, a product of The Jesus Movement, began to add local flavor to the church. Slaughter commonly brags about growing the church from an attendance of ninety to sixty-one in his first year; many of the congregants struggled with the changes he brought.

While some of the folks didn't have a palate for Mike's new recipe and were more comfortable with the one developed in

[11] *Super Size Me.* Directed by Morgan Spurlock. Performance by Morgan Spurlock. Samuel Goldwyn Films Roadside Attractions, 2004.

the 1950s, eventually word spread that there was something new happening, and the church grew to over 3,000 people gathering in a building surrounded by a cornfield. Ginghamsburg is located in an area that is 95 percent Caucasian, which made them strive to become more diverse.[12]

Even though at one time Roz worked at this megachurch, he knew that planting satellite campuses in urban areas didn't mean making Happy Meals. Ginghamsburg's second campus, Fort McKinley, was an urban restart in 2008. Fort McKinley is 53 percent African American.[13] In 2012, a third location called The Point launched in Trotwood, Ohio, whose demographics are close to 70 percent African American.[14] The meal prepared at the Tipp City campus looks different than the meal we cooked at the satellite campuses. They have left room for contextualization, providing a local flavor for their satellite communities by asking the people what they are truly hungry for in look, feel, and taste. For example, their campuses generally do the same sermon series, but there are times when the menu has to be tweaked to offer something different when sermons don't translate across the board.

The outreach and discipleship programs share similarities and the main DNA, but are nuanced to fit the context. The worship music follows a different set list at each campus, although there are times when songs are sung across all three locations on the same Sunday. The sermons generally use the same Scriptural text, but there is freedom to go in a different

---

[12] SuburbanStats.org, "Current Tipp City, Ohio Population, Demographics and Stats in 2017, 2018." www.suburbanstats.org/population/ohio/how-many-people-live-in-tipp-city. December 18, 2019.

[13] CityData.com. "Fort McKinley, Ohio." www.city-data.com/city/Fort-McKinley-Ohio.html. Accessed December 18, 2019.

[14] CityData.com. "Trotwood, Ohio." www.city-data.com/city/Trotwood-Ohio.html. Accessed December 18, 2019.

direction with unique illustrations and points. The preachers gather together to collaborate, but there is a freedom to decide what will meet the missional needs of their communities.

God has created unique faith communities for a reason. The reason is to find the local flavor and seasoning so that, like Ezra, all people can understand the meaning and come to the table.

What is the local flavor you can serve up to your people? On nearly every list of the best burger joints in Dayton, you'll find Tank's Bar and Grill near the top. Tank's isn't big or conspicuous, and it isn't very aggressive about marketing itself. It doesn't have to be; people love it. Business spreads by word of mouth, and it's often a surprise to people that a dive bar near downtown feeds people right. The burgers are out of this world.

What's the secret? The late owner Dan "Tank" Tankersley said it himself. "Fresh, fresh, fresh ... and the quality helps, too."[15] The ingredient list is a 100 percent whole-wheat bun and a 100 percent Grade A USDA Choice hamburger. Sounds a little different than that burger from McDonald's, doesn't it? A Tank's burger is locally sourced, and people come from all over the city to get one.[16]

The reason the show *Diners, Drive-Ins and Dives* is popular is because Guy Fieri finds places like Tank's. Yet, the places Guy visits aren't secrets to the locals, only to the out-of-towners. Guy never goes to a chain.

How do you do this at home? How do you move away from franchise thinking and toward becoming a local dive?

---

[15] The Food Adventures Crew, "The Top 35 Burgers of Dayton." *Dayton Most Metro,* www.mostmetro.com/dayton-dining/the-top-35-burgers-of-dayton.html. (May 22, 2015).

[16] Ibid.

The reason many of our churches are declining or dying is because the franchise model has become predetermined, predictable, and sterile. It lacks the heart of local, home-grown, farm-fresh ministry that uses real ingredients.

Friends, what are you serving up to your people to make disciples? We are people of flavor, which means getting local. Jesus himself said we are the salt of the earth. "Let me tell you why you are here. You're here to be the salt—seasoning that brings out the God-flavors of this earth. If you lose your saltiness, how will people taste godliness? You've lost your usefulness and will end up in the garbage" (Matthew 5:13, *The Message*). Nowhere in this text does Jesus say, "You ought...you should...you can be...you might try to be...." Jesus says, "You are." Whether we as God's people do it well or poorly, whether we intend it or not—we witness to Jesus. With our words and actions, our silence and our inaction, we let others know whether we believe that what Jesus said, did, and taught is true. Christians can't live as if our faith doesn't matter. Faith in Jesus leads to action, and our actions point to and help bring forth God's Kingdom.

Historically, salt was precious. It was used for many purposes. An important purpose was that it preserved food. People didn't have refrigeration, so salt kept food from rotting like the garbage. Salt also flavored food. It brought out the natural, good flavor of foods. As Christians, we are to bring out what is true and righteous in the world, and preserve it.

Christianity should be vibrant and visible. Salt in a salt-shaker, like light under a bushel basket, makes no impact. Christianity void of deeds of compassion influences no one. The Church is called to be creative in how it cooks a meal to feed the needs of people. Jesus tells us we are the salt of the earth and the light of the world. We are called to make a difference, not just look toward heaven. When we say the Lord's Prayer, we reflect heaven on earth as we pray, "Your Kingdom come, your will be done, on earth as it is in heaven" (Matthew 6: 10-11, NIV). More than just a prayer, this is a way of life. It's taking action. We are building the Kingdom of God every day. The Church is called to bring a foretaste of the Heavenly Banquet (Jesus described this in The Parable of The Wedding Feast in Matthew 22:1-14 and Luke 14:7-14) as John the Revelator describes in Revelation 19:7-9:

> *Let us rejoice and be glad*
> *and give him glory!*
> *For the wedding of the Lamb has come,*
> *and his bride has made herself ready.*
> *Fine linen, bright and clean,*
> *was given her to wear* (NIV).

We are called to bring out the flavor that's already there. Salt is only good when it's used to flavor a meal. Franchise dictates the flavor it serves: this is our flavor, take it or leave it. Local means figuring out what's already there and building on it. We are called to enhance the local flavor. Are we going to serve up the same thing week after week and expect different results, or are we going to choose to cook up something great in our communities?

If you accept the challenge, it is our prayer that this book will help leaders and churches find their own voices and transform their churches in a way that a franchise approach simply cannot accomplish. While churches can and should look to each other for best practices, we will also encourage churches to seek implementation from their own contexts.

One final note: In order to help process the ideas

presented in the book, we've written a series of reflection questions that will appear throughout each chapter. We encourage you to work through those on your own or with a group of leaders as you're reading.

CHAPTER 1

When you read the title of this book, you might think we're suggesting franchises are bad, and local dives are good. Let's be clear: Franchises aren't bad. In fact, for the most part, they are very good. Franchises are so good, they are worthy of expansion. They have a product, service, and style that is so effective, they can, and often even should, be replicated.

In Jason's work across the church, he has had the privilege of coaching, speaking at, visiting, and working with some of the most popular franchises in the (big "C") Church. Within United Methodism, he's been presented with opportunities to join the staff at several of the largest churches in the denomination and was employed at one of its flagship churches two decades ago.

The truth is, we love megachurches and those who have built them. Each one has done so many things right, and many have replicated, in whole or in part, some of the most inspiring aspects of their ministries. Megachurches understand excellence and quality in worship, hospitality, discipleship, community building, and mission. Most importantly, sustainable churches are rooted in the life-transforming power of Jesus Christ.

Megachurches have earned the right to franchise, and while they are a relatively new phenomenon, they have already left an indelible mark on Western Christianity. Decades ago, when the rise of megachurches began, virtually every denomination and religious group was experiencing a decline in attendance. The growth of the megachurch has defied the odds and the realities playing out as smaller churches all over the country were closing one by one.

So, what exactly is a megachurch? The Hartford Institute for Religion Research defines it like this: "The term megachurch generally refers to any Protestant Christian congregation with a sustained average weekly attendance of 2000 persons or more in its worship services, counting all adults and children at all its worship locations."[17]

With that many people involved, these churches had to iterate or die. Many of them focused on building systems, strengthening and expanding membership, creating discipleship pathways, building new spaces, and renovating old ones. The work of perfecting what they had was often at the heart of sustaining what was already built. In those years, when explosive growth was the norm, worship venues started to look more like concert halls or sports arenas. Houses of worship began including things like bookstores, coffee shops, and other spaces that mimicked retail stores at the local mall.

When the foundation was set, the next logical step was to begin planting new congregations. With so much success, it would seem logical to simply take the exact same recipe and move it to another part of town. However, this thinking is shortsighted and can be detrimental to the new faith community.

As some megachurches have added multi-site campuses, important components have sometimes been overlooked, specifically: contextualization, developing indigenous leaders, and incarnational ministry.

In the book Nehemiah, Ezra had, in a sense, come from an exclusive franchise. Had the Levites not come along to translate the law to the people in a language they understood—cook it up with local flavor—the locals could not have participated in the meal.

The Levites had to know the language of the people in order to translate their message into a language they could understand. The Levites must have been out amongst the people in the square enough that they knew how to move

[17] Hartford Institute for Religion Research, Megachurch Definition, http://hirr.hartsem.edu/megachurch/definition.html. Accessed December 18, 2019.

among them and use language that would eventually move the people to tears. In the act of translating the law, they modeled the local dive mentality.

Some satellites have failed because the franchised recipe missed the mark in a new setting. They may have come with experience, a strong brand, and excellent leadership, but also with the wrong recipe for the context. Failure may also stem from attempting to work outside of an established church's sweet spot.

Jorge Acevedo, a well-known and respected pastor, shared with us a valuable lesson learned when he tried to begin a new faith community that didn't take root. Jorge and his team at Grace Church have done incredible work in reviving several churches in southern Florida that have become campuses of Grace. You'd be hard-pressed to find a team with a better understanding of what it takes to rehab a church in need of new life than his. They specialize in finding contextual recipes that meet people where they are, so that they may come to know the transforming power of a life in Jesus Christ.[18]

At their central campus, Pastor Arlene Jackson did a remarkable job finding ways to bring a beloved recipe to the locals that has them coming back week after week. Under her leadership, the church grew from thirty to over three hundred. Clearly, she understands the local dive mentality.[19]

That makes the following story even more interesting. Arlene and her husband were feeling drawn to Sioux Falls, South Dakota. They wanted to live closer to their son. There was only one problem; they absolutely loved Grace Church and didn't want to leave.[20]

---

[18] Moore, Jason, and Jorge Acevedo. "Grace Church." Sept. 6, 2018.

[19] Ibid.

[20] Ibid.

Arlene thought, "Why not take Grace with us to Sioux Falls?" Being the top-notch leader she is, it wasn't long before that idea became a reality, and a partnership between The Dakotas Conference of The United Methodist Church and Grace Church was formed. After much prayer, planning, and preparation, the church launched in November of 2015.[21]

With the support of the conference, Arlene and her team found a location, brought the DNA of Grace to the new worship experience, and gave it a valiant effort. While there were some really great things happening during the months that Grace Sioux Falls was a worshiping faith community, the church failed to ignite. In April of the following year, the church closed.[22]

Upon reflection, the leadership team at Grace admitted that they hadn't fully understood the context of Sioux Falls before they got there. They also had historically been "rehab addicts," rather than church starters. Grace's sweet spot has always been that of taking a faith community that is in need of new life, infusing it with transformational core values and practices, and allowing those communities to discover what works in their indigenous context.[23]

Also at the heart of Grace Church is recovery ministry. It's part of everything they do, and it's an area of passion for Arlene. As it turns out, two well-established recovery ministries were already happening in the same basic location where Grace Sioux Falls was situated. This made gaining a foothold even more challenging.[24]

---

[21] Ibid.

[22] Ibid.

[23] Ibid.

[24] Ibid.

Reflection Questions:

If you are considering planting a new faith community, or reformulating your recipe for a new place, do you know what to expect when you get there?

Are you attempting to live outside of your sweet spot?

Jorge shared another valuable reflection that he heard recently at a conference led by Andy Stanley at the Global Leadership Summit in 2017. Andy said, "What are you uniquely better at? Build your ministry around that."[25] There may be others in the area where you hope to plant who are uniquely better at whatever it is you plan to do. Or maybe they have it already established before you arrived, so that there isn't a demand for what you offer.

Grace Sioux Falls had a great leader at the helm, plenty of funding, a great brand, excellent DNA, but their "uniquely better" was rooted in recovery ministry and rehabbing rather than starting something from scratch. With other ministries in place prior to their arrival, "uniquely better" was going to be an uphill battle, and to top it off, they were attempting to build from scratch rather than rehab.[26]

Still, God is faithful. Arlene returned to Florida, and Grace continues to have a tremendous impact on the ministry there.[27]

---

[25] Ibid.

[26] Ibid.

[27] Ibid.

While there are aspects of Grace Church that mimic the feel of a franchise, they model the local dive ethos at their various campuses. Jorge functions much like a mentor and coach to the lead pastors at each campus, rather than an enforcer who dictates how each campus will carry out his plan.[28]

They meet as a team to develop outlines for series and themes, but each pastor has the freedom to carry out the message in whatever style fits. Some are more experiential preachers, while others deliver a less frilly, straight-up style of teaching.

The leadership at Grace has developed an extensive playbook to assure that everyone is on the same page. The playbook includes: vision, values, strategy, structure, and theology. These non-negotiables set the standards accordingly by which each campus can cook up their local meals.

When it's decision time and questions arise around how things will play out at the various campuses, Jorge says there are two things to consider: the playbook and the preferences. The **playbook** names some specific strategies: *what they all agree to putting on the menu*, and the **preferences**: *what seasonings, toppings, and sides will be added to the agreed-upon meal.*[29]

Jorge sometimes puts it like this:

The McDonald's near SeaWorld serves Big Macs, fries, and shakes. The building is decorated with Shamu and other aquatic animals. The McDonald's outside of Disney World, serves Big Macs, fries, and shakes. The store is decorated with

[28] Ibid.

[29] Ibid.

Mickey, Minnie, Donald, and Goofy. The McDonald's near Lego Land serves Big Macs, fries, and shakes. It's decorated with Lego characters.[30]

As long as Big Macs, fries, and shakes are on the menu, you can do whatever you prefer for the décor. There is both consistency and freedom in this approach. It's the best of franchise and local dive. The guiding strategies are a must, but what they look like can be highly contextual.

Those core strategies are:

Reach: Ministries that engage and invite unchurched people in our community to experience the love of Jesus through the body of Christ. "Go to the street corners and invite to the banquet anyone you find" Matthew 22:9 (NIV).

Connect: Ministries that help people connect to Jesus and the Grace Church family.

All the believers devoted themselves to the apostles' teaching, and to fellowship, and to sharing in meals (including the Lord's Supper), and to prayer .... They worshiped together at the Temple each day, met in homes for the Lord's Supper, and shared their meals with great joy and generosity—all the while praising God and enjoying the goodwill of all the people. And each day the Lord added to their fellowship those who were being saved" Acts 2:42, 46-47 (NLT).

Form: Ministries that help people have a growing and transforming relationship with Jesus Christ. "And yet, O Lord, you are our Father. We are the clay, and you are the potter. We all are formed by your hand" Isaiah 64:8 (NLT).

Send: Ministries that release God's people to make the realities of heaven the realities of earth.

---

[30] Ibid.

> *"Again Jesus said, 'Peace be with you! As the Father has sent me, I am sending you'"* John 20:20-22 (NIV).[31]

Reflection Question:

What are your core values and how might they allow freedom for churches you may plant?

Let's further define *franchisor* and *franchisee* to better understand the relationship between the two. In the world of business, Entrepreuer.com defines the relationship like this:

> *Generally speaking, a franchisee is someone who pays a franchisor an initial franchise fee, averaging close to $30,000 in today's market, for the right to operate a business under the franchisor's name using the franchisor's business model. The franchisee furnishes all the capital required for opening the business and assumes full financial and operational responsibility for running the business. The franchisee generally will also pay a continuing royalty (usually between 4 and 10 percent of gross sales, or even higher) to the franchisor, and often the franchisee will buy products from the franchisor.*[32]

In the church, the relationship is structured very differently. While much of what defines the franchisor/franchisee relationship does not apply, there are important parallels. In

---

[31] Grace Playbook, Updated March 2016.

[32] Siebert, M. *The Rules and Regulations of Being a Franchisor.* Retrieved from www.entrepreneur.com, December 2, 2015.

our scenario, the franchisor is providing most, if not all, of the financing for the franchisee to launch. This is a contrast.

A similarity is that, in many cases, the franchisor is going to provide branding support and possibly a name, business model, and administrative functions. And while there are no royalties involved, the income derived from the franchisee (tithes and offerings) is likely going to funnel back to the franchisor.

There are tensions that can quickly rear up when the relationship isn't clearly defined in the beginning. It is important that there is a clear understanding by all parties as to how the two entities will operate.

For instance, will the look/feel and brand identity carry over from one site to another, or will each have its own indigenous identity? In other words, will this be Acme Church, Acme Church North, Acme Church South? Or might it be Acme Church and respectively Wile E. Coyote Church: A campus of Acme Church? Or might there be no name connection whatsoever?

Will the campuses be offering the same message series? Or do they do their own thing? How much contextualization is welcome versus how much carrying forth of the planting church is mandated?

There is no wrong answer to these questions. We have coached and worked with churches that have made all of those scenarios work well. We've also coached and worked with churches who have struggled because there wasn't enough structure and understanding agreed upon in the beginning. In chapter 3, we'll give you some tools to work through these concerns. The lack of doing so leads to resentment, misunderstandings, and distrust.

While every franchisor/franchisee relationship is

different, and not everything is known at the beginning, the more clarity that can be reached at the start, the easier it is to deal with misalignments as they happen.

Consider developing a letter of intent between the franchisor and the franchisee. In chapter 3, we get into the nitty gritty of what should be included.

A letter of intent (or covenant agreement) can be a living document that guides the relationship as it evolves. Its purpose is to create a common understanding of what is or isn't, as Grace Church puts it, "Part of the Playbook" or "preference."

When Jason helped plant a church in the Dayton area nearly two decades ago, the team he was a part of and the planting church regularly experienced tension when carrying out their respective ministries. The planting church, Stillwater United Methodist Church, was doing vibrant ministry with an experienced and beloved leader. The church was strong, growing, and ready to expand and try something new. A team formed to plant a new congregation at the local YMCA. The idea was that Stillwater would be "one church in two locations." On paper, the tagline had a nice ring. Living it out was a different story.

Unfortunately, missteps were made right from the beginning in the naming of this new faith community. Brilliantly, the new church was called "Living Water." When isolated, that name sounds fresh and meaningful. One only has to consider that the name of the planting church was called "Stillwater," and maybe you can see the problem. They were both alive and moving, but it almost appeared as if the plant was claiming the new thing was living and the old one was dead.

Both churches set out to do their thing, and when there was freedom and autonomy to do what worked best for the respective communities, everything worked pretty well. Stillwater had a great worship process, team, pastor, staff, and congregation, and Living Water was building toward those things, too.

The challenges came when the two would attempt church-wide videos, series, announcements, and events. Because both locations had very different audiences, and even worship styles, bands, and media standards, when the main campus would mandate a video be shown or an announcement be made at the satellite campus, it would feel out of sync and confusing for those who had never been to the main campus. This would often create conflict because Jason and the team resisted anything that didn't fit where Living Water was going strategically.

Further complications arose when the two worship design teams would get together to plan joint services like Christmas and Easter. Because each team had its own processes and personalities, there wasn't much safe space, which made collaboration hard. More often than not, there was a collective sense that it was more trouble than it was worth to force it. In time, during that season, it became better for each campus to cook its own recipe.

Both churches are still going strong, and the YMCA church was wisely renamed "Stillwater at the Y" years ago.

One church in two locations, or three or four, is an exciting notion, but one that is difficult to make a reality. It can be done, but it has to be done right. Without some very intentional work upfront, it can be detrimental to a proper launch and long-term sustainability.

Reflection Questions:

What are some of the non-negotiables that your local dive must include in its recipe?

How much autonomy is to be given?

How should you name your local dive?

It is of utmost importance when it comes to extending and developing a personal relationship with Christ to a community made up of individuals, that we recognize a one size-fits-all approach to ministry will inevitably leave some hungry.

Ezra and those who could read the law had full bellies and could partake of the meal any time they wanted. The people gathered who had never tasted this meal couldn't participate in it until the Levites cooked it up in their context.

The established church (franchisor) may have a completely different constituency than the satellite (franchisee), even if they are just across town from one another. While the two (or more) may share zip codes, a different recipe may be required to connect.

In the same way that international missionaries prepare to travel to another country to serve a foreign culture, so must we invest in learning what a community's customs are all about. What are the individuals in that community hungry for? The answers aren't always easy to find.

It has been said that the best way to learn a foreign language is to live in a place where that language is natively spoken. This immersion is also part of what makes for a successful local dive.

THE GATHERING, ST. LOUIS

In a recent conversation with our friend Matt Miofsky, planter and founding pastor of The Gathering in Saint Louis, Matt said, "There are some things you can't learn from a demographic report. While www.missioninsite.com is a valuable resource, it doesn't tell the whole story. There's much more at play than what is on paper."[33]

Immersing oneself in a community is very important. For the leadership at The Gathering, it is an essential core value. Matt is adamant that campus pastors have an intimate connection to the place where they're planting. In fact, their present strategy is to find longtime residents—whether they are lay or clergy—to lead new sites.[34]

Matt says, "When we put people in places they understand, there is a higher degree of success."[35] He also points out that many of the most successful, rapidly growing, and sustainable churches are led by pastors who planted in the area they are from or where they have spent significant time. "When you consider what's happened at places like Ginghamsburg UMC with Mike Slaughter, Saddleback with Rick Warren, Embrace with Adam Weber, Church of the Resurrection with Adam Hamilton, and other large churches, you can see how having a home-grown connection has an impact."[36] Matt points out that other churches that have grown like wildfire and sustained

[33] Moore, Jason, and Matt Miofsky. "The Gathering." Sept 6. 2018.

[34] Ibid.

[35] Ibid.

[36] Ibid.

their growth, have pastors who have adopted their cities and have become like natives.

One of the worst mistakes a planting pastor can bring is the mentality that this is a short- term assignment, or that they're just learning from this experience for their next one. Miofsky says, "You have to plant a new faith community with the mindset that you're going to be there forever. Having a 'this is a temporary appointment' mentality is detrimental to its success. People can sniff out someone who is only passing through."[37]

There is a tension that must be held in balance as franchisors think about who should lead their local dives. Talent goes a long way, but having that indigenous connection to a community is like the secret sauce that brings something special to a local dive.

Local flavor is always going to matter, no matter where you take the franchise, but the more you take the franchise to places that are similar to where you begin, the easier it is going to be to adapt the recipe. The Gathering has several sites and is in the process of launching another location. Matt emphasizes that a church that wants to plant has to be self-aware enough to admit who they really are and where they can truly be effective. He says,

> *We had to be really honest with ourselves. There are places where we don't think our values are a match. These are the places we have no intention of going. We know we're an urban church. It would be really hard for us to develop a recipe that would work in a suburban setting. Our church grew up in the city.*[38]

All of The Gathering's sites are four or five miles away from each other. They're very similar contextually. This

---

[37] Ibid.

[38] Ibid.

doesn't mean that the recipe is the same. But Matt says, "We have very few hard and fast rules. There is a lot of room to contextualize."[39] The Gathering's recipe works because they use indigenous leaders and places where the context is very similar. Similar demographics and sensibilities, and native leaders are a one-two punch that makes it all work.

Instead of looking at a population growth study and blindly planting a church in the center of a hot zone, it's important to ask if there is an affinity for what's happening there for the church that is looking to go to that location. This only happens with immersion in the context.

Reflection Questions:

Do your leaders have a local connection? If not, can they learn to love, assimilate into, and become a part of the community you're planting in?

Does the dream location for your local dive match up with who you are and your values?

Are you compatible with the area?

You may find that another area just a short drive away is better than planting two cities over. You may also find that a native, bi-vocational pastor, or layperson from the area is

[39] Ibid.

a better choice than a headhunter-selected superstar from another region. On the other hand, with intentionality, an outsider can integrate into a community.

One of the pastors Matt Miofsky lifts up as an example of someone who has done this is pastor Scott Chrostek. Scott is the founding pastor of Church of the Resurrection's downtown campus.

Scott is originally from Detroit, a city that has gone through some very difficult challenges in the past several decades. Changes in the auto industry have led to a decline in manufacturing jobs. This has left the city feeling beat down, with a depressed view of the future.[40] Kansas City, where Scott lives now, is a city where there is a palpable sense of hope and prosperity. For Scott, this was a breath of fresh air, but it also meant getting in touch with a very different ethos.[41]

RESURRECTION DOWNTOWN, KANSAS CITY, KS

While two large cities might have some of the same things in common—busy traffic, a bustling downtown, great food, entertainment districts—there are many ways that larger cities differ from one another. Scott points out that each city has a personality, and a planter has to be intentional about getting to know the personality of their city.[42] "A planter has to develop an honest eagerness about learning what the community is

[40] Moore, Jason, and Scott Chrostek. "The Church of The Resurrection-Downtown Campus." Sept. 7, 2018.

[41] Ibid.

[42] Ibid.

like. Living in the community is a must. You have a much greater chance of running into your neighbors when you live in the neighborhood than you do when you commute in."[43]

From day one, Scott and his wife moved into an apartment in the heart of downtown Kansas City. It was a foundational part of his strategy for planting a new faith community. As the church has grown, moved, and even built a new building, Scott has remained in the city.[44]

One of the most impressive things about this is that Scott's mother church is the United Methodist Church of the Resurrection in Leawood, Kansas. It is the largest church in the denomination, and is seated in one of the fastest growing neighborhoods in a suburb about thirty minutes away.[45] With staff meetings and preaching responsibilities at the main campus from time to time, it might be easier to live in the suburb and drive in to downtown when he needs to be there. But that's not how Scott has built a winning recipe.[46]

As far as franchises go, Church of the Resurrection has "a brand" that is known nationwide. Its founding and senior pastor is Reverend Adam Hamilton. Hamilton started the congregation in 1990. Hamilton is committed to the renewal of the mainline church, especially the United Methodist Church. In 2012, he was invited by the White House to deliver the message at the National Prayer Service as a part of President Obama's second inauguration.[47]

---

[43] Ibid.

[44] Ibid.

[45] Ibid.

[46] Ibid.

[47] "United Methodist Church of the Resurrection." Wikipediat.org. https://en.wikipedia.org/wiki/United_Methodist_Church_of_the_Resurrection. Accessed December 18, 2019.

Resurrection is a church worthy of replicating, and they've taken a number of different approaches to creating the local dive experience in other communities. Each of their four campuses was started with a different approach. Some started out with a sort of missionary congregation supplied by the main campus, while others were seeded with fewer people and built up from the local area. Scott's location had a small team from the main campus, but was mainly cultivated from people within the community.[48]

Church of the Resurrection has a strong motivation not to create a cookie-cutter experience, but places an emphasis on maintaining a shared clarity of purpose. A lot of work is done to infuse the DNA of the main campus into the other sites. An unwavering commitment to shared vision allows for lots of opportunities to be unique and distinct. While each local dive serves up its own kind of fare, you'll sense the vision and values at each location.[49]

Scott shared with us that one of the most valuable aspects of customizing the recipe was starting with a small team.

> *When you start with a pastor, worship leader and a ten-hour-a-week administrator, you are pushed to a place where you are reliant on volunteers. Everything from music, to mission opportunities, education and more is owned by the people in the community. When we began adding staff, most of them came from within the worshiping congregation or from the downtown area. This really helped us create a sense of local flavor.*[50]

There are campus pastors at each of Church of the Resurrection's locations, but the majority of the time they use

---

[48] Moore, Jason, and Scott Chrostek. "The Church of The Resurrection-Downtown Campus." Sept. 7, 2018.

[49] Ibid.

[50] Ibid.

Adam's sermon on video from the main campus during their worship. We asked Scott how local context has been brought to that methodology.[51]

First, Scott said that the video venue was invaluable in allowing time for relationship building within the community. "In the same time twenty hours I could spend developing a sermon that would be heard by maybe 200 people early on, I could be out meeting over 200 new people who were not yet with us," said Scott.[52] His job was really to do the work of building Christian community, and launching the campus. The video venue allowed for more time to do that.

Scott said, "Relationships trumped having live preaching."[53] The role of the site pastor is important in contextualizing what's being shared from the screen. The congregation has an established familiarity with the site pastor that sets up what is heard in the message. The site pastor also is intentionally helping people understand the connection to Church of the Resurrection's shared mission, purpose, vision, and journey each week.

Second, on the weeks Scott does preach live, he doesn't retreat to his office for sermon writing. Instead, he elects to find a coffee shop somewhere downtown. Scott says, "When I write my sermons, I write them in local coffee shops. It's not efficient by any means because I get interrupted and end up in multiple conversations with people, but it's one of the intentional ways I stay connected to my community."[54]

Being out in the community allows you to lap up the local

---

[51] Ibid.

[52] Ibid.

[53] Ibid.

[54] Ibid.

flavor in meaningful ways. It also creates opportunities for conversations with people who are not yet in your church. Another part of Scott's winning recipe is to set a goal for the number of people he wants to talk to in a day, then track and measure it. Surface level, impromptu ice-breaking conversations can become invaluable listening sessions. The things gained in conversations like Scott's allow you to learn about the city and the people in it. As Scott says, "The people shape the city."[55]

When Church of the Resurrection decided to "franchise," it didn't impose the city of Leawood on downtown Kansas City. Instead, through Scott and his team, they got to know the city and the people, and created a recipe that works for that area.

Reflection Questions:

What are you doing to "live in the city" where your local dive is or will be?

Are you creating opportunities for interruptions, and impromptu conversations?

A franchise that does not think local is bound to serve up something that is out of touch, contrived, and poorly received. What may work in one place might fail to catch fire in another. In the next chapter we'll dig deeper into what local dives are all about.

---

[55] Ibid.

CHAPTER 2

ORGANIC COMMUNITIES

Authentic Christian community can't be manufactured in rows. It happens in circles. New expressions of church are cropping up everywhere. These micro-churches often take place in "third spaces" like house churches, coffeehouses, restaurants, and breweries. What does it look like for existing churches, regardless of their size, to get in touch with the local flavor? It means finding the ingredients that already exist in a given community and contextualizing ministry to meet specific needs. The franchise model fails to recognize, appreciate, and make use of these ingredients that are so readily available right in our own neighborhoods.

Consider the story of Normal Heights United Methodist Church just outside of San Diego, California. Founded in 1913, it experienced seasons of rapid growth and eventually decline. In its heyday, Normal Heights had over 700 members and a bustling Sunday school program. As often happens, attendance started to dwindle, and, out of necessity, the church became part of a cooperative parish of six other United Methodist churches. This was done so the churches could share resources and celebrate a like-minded connection.

NORMAL HEIGHTS UMC, NORMAL HEIGHTS, CA

In a sense, the United Methodist Church is like a franchise. There are common books of worship, hymnals, liturgies, a denomination-wide book of discipline, shared organizational structures, and more. Normal Heights UMC participated in these practices for years, and for a number of seasons did well to serve up a franchise recipe that was still palatable to the people in its context.

As growth eventually gave way to plateau, then decline, the church recognized a need for a new recipe. In 2012, with a focus on becoming more community-minded, Nancy Palmer, a community organizer and event planner, was hired to arrange movie nights, children's play groups, and other community-based activities.

A year later when pastor Brent Ross was appointed, he brought a style of worship he'd been developing at his previous church for the past eighteen months. He intuited that his recipe would have to change to translate to this new setting.

Brent began meeting with people from the community to build relationships and learn about the local flavor. Honest conversations about which practices, rituals, and activities connected and which didn't led to the further development of the recipe he'd been working on. This both honored previous worship at Normal Heights, but also focused on the present and future.

Brent's prophetic voice is rooted in a move away from what he calls "the sage from the stage," to becoming more of an initiator of a sacred conversation. People connect with Brent's voice because it's real—deep but not lofty, accessible but not simple. The worship experience names this ethos in its moniker, "Sacred Ordinary."

In Sacred Ordinary worship, the pews have been arranged in a circle, rather than in long rows with an aisle down the center. The band plays amongst the people, who face inward, rather than standing in a row facing people like a concert performance. Scripture is read from the pews by laypeople. On what was once the chancel and altar area, people spread out comfortably, sitting on the floor and the steps that once led to a choir loft.

White Christmas lights dangle above the gathering. Projectors throw lyrics and other images on the side walls of the church. The updated in-the-round arrangement provides an easy view from any seat in the house of the responsive prayers, scripture, and other liturgies being projected.

The experience begins with a worship focus, setting the foundation for the day. This is followed by music and then a time of "community opportunities." This isn't just a list regurgitated from the bulletin, but includes happenings inside and outside the life of the church. You're just as likely to hear about the local street fair as you are to hear about the Bible study that happens prior to worship each week.

Next follows an extended community time. This isn't a run-of-the-mill passing of the peace, or a cringe-inducing "awkwardly greet your neighbor" time. Instead, participants are artfully and intentionally invited to one of several options ranging from sitting in one's seat for a moment of self-reflection, to moving to a far corner where candles and a representation of the Western Wall in Jerusalem are at the ready. Worshipers are given a description of what these things are and what they represent. They are invited to light a candle or write a prayer and place it between the cracks of the wall's stones.

At the midpoint of the sanctuary is mounted a framed fabric bulletin board and opposite it is a table with paper hearts and pens. This station is an intercessory prayer station, though that would likely not be the word worship leaders would use to describe it. One Sunday, worshipers were asked to pray for baby Grace who had been born one month premature. A prayer for Grace could be written on a heart and pinned to the fabric board with a paper clip. Private prayers could be attached to the board, writing side faced down, so the pastors and staff team could pray over those anonymous prayers later in the week.

In what was originally the back of the room, a large chalkboard is emblazoned with a weekly question that ties to the sermon. One week its bold hand-written chalk letters read, "What does the Kingdom of God look like?" Children could find markers, colored pencils, crayons, and paper there to illustrate the question of the day. Adults who might prefer to engage through art were invited to pick up a canvas and provided paints to take notes through a painting or other artistic expression.

Still others might choose to move out to the welcome area for a cupcake or a cup of coffee. An eclectic collection of colorful mugs like you'd find in someone's cupboard are spread out and ready to be filled with one of several locally sourced coffee options.

"Conversation Spaces" are marked under the stairwells that lead up to the balcony. Attendees are careful to watch their steps, as the community basset hound and pug pleasantly roam the area.

When community time comes to an end, the people re-gather, and a message is offered. Brent uses common language, parable, and current connections to make his point. The goal is to bring the ordinary into the sacred and take the sacred back home to the ordinary. Communion is served weekly and is a ritual that is given meaning and context for regulars and visitors alike.

Scan across the room, and you'll see people from all walks

of life filling the pews—every age group imaginable from children to retirement age, soccer moms, hipsters, and a range of people from various socioeconomic backgrounds—coming together for a time of deep, meaningful worship. With the doors and windows open to the outside, passersby might think it looks more like friends gathered in a living room than a church. The music sounds more like a Mumford & Sons performance than the contemporary music on K-LOVE.

The experience isn't easy to categorize. It doesn't fit into a "traditional" or "contemporary" box, yet it's a recipe that has grown the church, its people, and its reputation in the community. This local dive is one that people walk, bike, and Uber to because it's a recipe that is grown out of the context of its own neighborhood.[56]

Reflection Questions:

How might reconfiguring your space create more of a sense of community?

What can you do to bring the ordinary into the sacred, and the sacred into the ordinary throughout the week?

Can your church live outside the standard categories of "traditional," "contemporary," and "blended" worship?

In Ezra's context in Nehemiah chapter 8, we see that the revival did not break out in a temple, church service, or religious festival. It happened outside at a time that nobody

[56] Ross, Brent. 2018 Interview by author. August 29, 2018.

suspected. It was one of the first open air revivals we see in the Scriptures. The other interesting thing we see in this chapter is that it isn't necessarily Ezra's agenda to hold this spontaneous church service. Instead, the people initiate it. Nehemiah 8:1 says, "... all the people came together as one in the square before the Water Gate. They told Ezra the teacher of the Law to bring out the Book of the Law of Moses, which the Lord had commanded for Israel" (NIV). Ezra was told to bring the Scriptures out. It was unplanned, and when Ezra stood up to the platform, the Holy Spirit took over. It was organically led, not from a model of top-down leadership but from the bottom up. The attraction of the day was not spectacular music, a charismatic speaker, the latest and greatest technology, or trendy building architecture. It was simply God's Word. It happened on the local level, and the scribes were made available to help the people understand what was being spoken.

One of the biggest and most innovative franchises in the world is Apple. Apple now holds more than a trillion dollars in assets and shares. Yet, even this colossally successful operation can make mistakes when it fails to contextualize. In 2017, Apple was opening a store on the Magnificent Mile in Chicago. One of the trademarks of an Apple Store is excellent customer service in an environment that is full of light, and, on the outside, a structure surrounded by glass rather than opaque walls. However, Apple failed to take into consideration Chicago's winter climate in the design of this particular store. The result was costly cracks to the exterior that continued to ripple through the glass. The replacement glass had to be stronger to withstand the cold weather, and came at a higher price than initially anticipated. While Apple won't struggle to absorb the monetary cost of the Chicago window fiasco, this points out that even the best organizations run into setbacks when they forget to contextualize.[57]

A local dive that Roz has become partial to (and not just because it shares a name with his daughter) is Lily's Bistro in downtown Dayton, Ohio's historic Oregon District. Lily's is an eclectic, independently-owned restaurant known for its brunch and dinner menus. Lily's works with other small business owners to source fresh ingredients for its menu and partners with local growers to serve a rotating farm-to-table daily menu. Any given visit to Lily's leaves you wondering what creative dishes the chef will come up with next to serve at the popular restaurant. Many restaurants cannot offer a daily rotating menu, but Lily's has found a way to master it. The combination of fresh food, ingredients, and creativity is what has made Lily's a household name in Dayton. The atmosphere is also welcoming, even when the restaurant fills up. The small setting makes guests feel like they are eating a meal in their own living room. It has become a place where community happens organically. They have tapped into the local needs of the community to become successful.

While Lily's could certainly expand into a franchise if they desired, they have consciously made the decision to be in one place and do it the best they can. They believe if they franchised it would take away from their unique dining experience in their current setting.

Lily's Bistro's unapologetic local approach has allowed them to continue their entrepreneurial spirit with creativity.[58] For example, they started an event called "Pooches and Punches" to benefit a local pet adoption center. Owner Emily

---

[57] Koziarz, Jay. "New Mag Mile Apple Store Struggles with Falling Ice, Cracking Windows." *Curbed Chicago*, www.chicago.curbed.com/2017/12/29/16830266/michigan-avenue-apple-store-winter-ice-cracked-windows, December 29, 2017.

[58] *Lily's Bistro*, lilysbistro.com. Accessed December 9, 2019.

Mendenhall said, "Having the sidewalk patio open for dogs all the time is a perfect setting for summer events like this."[59] The event helped bring together a special punch drink mixed up by the bartender along with complimentary gourmet dog treats to satisfy the pets and their owners. Lily's has captured local partnership and how people in our current culture love having their dogs with them in more places than at home or the park.[60]

We've explored two dramatically different stories. First, we saw what can happen when an organization in franchise mode fails to contextualize. Second, we saw how a local dining establishment that recognizes both the resources available and the heartfelt needs of its patrons has become a staple in the community.

We want to say upfront that just because a church or a business has a franchise model doesn't automatically discredit the quality of service and care it provides to its congregation or customers. After all, we're both huge Apple fans and look to them for best practices all the time. A local dive or local congregation who operates out of meeting the needs in its community doesn't automatically translate to success either. It all comes down to the end goal and the process for getting there. As you consider your next move, consider these two examples: (1) what happened when the franchise mentality like Apple's fails to contextualize and (2) how a local dining establishment has become a staple in the community that recognizes the heartfelt needs of its patrons.

There are many advantages to the franchise model. If a company, church, or restaurant is operating successfully,

---

[59] "Where My Dogs at? Lily's Hosts Pet-Friendly Event," Dayton.com , www.dayton.com/news/local/where-dogs-lily-hosts-pet-friendly-event/kgaknOdQyKYcqOMgP-LoNCK/, August 13, 2016,

[60] Ibid.

franchising to expand the operations and efforts of reaching more people can be appealing. It is likely that the franchise model has more capital or funding than the local dive. A growing business can leverage profits, equity, and credit to their advantage. This allows franchises to recruit better talent. People are drawn to meaning and purpose and want to be part of something that's making an impact, no matter what it is. Also, there is room in the budget to incentivize employees who are exceeding expectations.

One example we see in the church world is the salary average that a multi-site megachurch can afford to pay compared to that of a local congregation. Other aspects like geography and cost of living factor in, but megachurches can afford to pay top dollar for talent in order to attract people who will be invested in the church and stay for a longer period of time.

Additionally, if the original model is working, the argument can be made that the operation should expand to a franchise. If there is a critical mass of people and there are resources, systems, and name recognition in place, it's easier to obtain a loan or startup money. Proven success means less risk taken. This increases an organization's opportunity to grow more, minimizing growth risk. A sound business plan and the variability of context can determine what type of risk is involved. The opportunity for return and growth can outweigh the risk taken. If these factors sound good to you, a franchise model of growth might be suitable.[61]

However, as with any model there are drawbacks. A franchise's bottom line is the profit margin, and this may not be your organization's end goal. Scott Shane, an entrepreneurial professor at Case Western Reserve University, says,

---

[61] Shane, Scott. "The Pros and Cons of Franchising Your Business," *Entrepreneur*, www.entrepreneur.com/article/226489, May 7, 2013.

Franchisors make money by collecting a percentage of sales as a royalty for letting the franchisee use their brand name and operating system. Franchisees make money from the outlet's profits. Anything that boosts sales, but not profits will create conflict between you and the franchisee. If you want to offer customers promotional coupons, franchisees may likely object. Coupons boost sales, but not always profits, benefiting the franchisor, but not necessarily the franchisee.[62]

When applied to the context of the church, a franchise model that is not paying for itself in sufficient time, lacks blockbuster growth numbers, or shows any sign of stagnation is often considered less successful than the original campus.

Another downside for churches is a failure to diversify. The financial officers of the original church or business often wish to reduce risk. They study demographics, average household income, and projected population growth to determine where to launch their next store or church. Resources like missioninsite.com are helpful in gathering this data. Often, those communities and contexts are similar to the original church or business location. The areas that are often overlooked are rural and urban areas. If a congregation is predominately middle class to upper middle class, it is likely that a second site would begin in a similar context.

This has been Roz's experience as he has studied churches around the country that have applied a franchise mentality to their multiplication. There is a small chance to have any ethnic diversity in the mix when replicating a formula reaching a homogeneous population. The sad thing about this is that it takes away from the vision of the

---

[62] Ibid.

Kingdom of God that Christ called the church to build on earth in the first place.

Many foundational scriptures address this, perhaps most importantly, Revelation 7:9: "After this I looked, and there before me was a great multitude that no one could count, from every nation, tribe, people and language, standing before the throne and before the Lamb. They were wearing white robes and were holding palm branches in their hands" (NIV). The church is called to reflect a picture of heaven. The franchise model can make it harder to live into that vision. The two factors that are overlooked in this model are ethnic and economic diversity. This is a great challenge for many churches to get their minds around, but when we over-subscribe to having to limit our planning toward a target audience, we can lose a sense of what makes up the Kingdom of God. Jesus is clear in his qualifier for his audience while starting his public ministry on earth. It's found in what many scholars call his inaugural address in Luke 4:18-19 (NIV):

The Spirit of the Lord is on me,
because he has anointed me
to proclaim good news to the poor.
He has sent me to proclaim freedom for the prisoners
and recovery of sight for the blind,
to set the oppressed free,
to proclaim the year of the Lord's favor.

The ministry of Jesus' shows us that he had a wide audience from the wealthy to those in poverty. Jesus crossed ethnic, social, religious, and fiscal barriers to carry out the work. As a church planter and leader, when Roz was asked in the past if he had a target audience for his congregation, people were surprised when he said that everyone is his target because everyone is deserving of the gospel. He understands that some churches have their own unique callings and giftings to reach different people. However, he wouldn't disqualify anyone or boast about who his target demographic is as a church.

The slogan of the most recent church Roz planted along with co-pastor Wayne Botkin, Mosaic Church in Dayton, Ohio, is "Better Together." Roz and Wayne believe that all people make up God's mosaic. God is bringing the nations to Dayton, and Mosaic is strategically positioned to reach people who are coming into the U.S.

MOSAIC CHURCH, BEAVERCREEK, OH

Dayton has become known as an open city where refugees and immigrants come to find a home. In 2011, then Mayor Leitzell and then City Manager Tim Riordan started a Friendly Immigrant City Initiative. Of the more than 300 U.S. cities with populations of 100,000 or more, only a handful have experienced a faster percentage growth in their foreign-born populations than Dayton. Since the mid-2000s, Dayton's immigrant population has roughly doubled to more than 7,000 people in 2016, according to Census data. In September 2015, the White House launched its Welcoming Communities campaign to better connect federal resources with local immigrant-friendly initiatives. Dayton was one of forty early adopter communities. Dayton Mayor Nan Whaley joined other mayors from across the country to sign a joint letter from Cities United for Immigration Action to the Obama Administration expressing their willingness to assist in the relocation process during the Syrian refugee crisis. All of this shows the community commitment to refugees and immigrants coming into Dayton, Ohio.[63]

The question the leaders of Mosaic Church asked themselves was how Mosaic Church would reach out to this need. They decided that one of their first staff hires would be an International Pastor. Some questioned this decision, not understanding the need to source such a position, but Mosaic felt it was crucial to live into what God was calling them to do. They were blessed to bring on a pastor from Egypt. In less than a year, the international pastor started a Bible study completely in Arabic with more than fifty people in attendance on Friday evenings. He has also started an international group with eleven different nations represented. Out of his evangelistic heart the church is starting English as a Second Language (ESL) classes and launching a new ministry called Arab Community Fellowship (ACF). One of ACF's goals is to create an inviting place that facilitates meetings where people can ask questions and offer potential solutions in a non-threatening atmosphere, while enjoying the fellowship of other Arabs. We believe Arab-speaking people will be better able to make decisions and develop friendships with both Arab and non-Arab-speaking people when they have better information. Through Ayad and Mosaic Church's work with refugees and immigrants, the church has realized that there are two primary keys to fitting into the American culture: first, learning the English language and second, an integration of the customs and values of American culture with one's own native traditions. The approach to the meetings is straightforward and simple. At the gatherings people can expect opportunities to discuss how to adapt to the culture in the U.S. by discussing problems and learning from those who have faced similar issues, meet new friends, participate in Bible studies,

---

[63] "About: Welcome Dayton Immigrant Friendly City Home Comments," www.welcomedayton.org/about/. Accessed December 18, 2019.

and enjoy fellowship and refreshments.

If Mosaic was locked into a franchise mentality and overlooked the opportunities staring them in the face, they wouldn't have been able to boldly engage in this new endeavor.

Mosaic's original parent churches, Ginghamsburg UMC and Christ Church in Kettering, Ohio, are situated in suburban communities with many established ministries in place. While the parent churches also share a desire to reach people of other nationalities, the effort to start an entirely new ministry with the focus described above would have been difficult. Mosaic began from scratch with this recipe at the core of its DNA. The parent churches provided the opportunities and means to cook a recipe that would be difficult to initiate or maintain within their original congregations.

Many times, the franchise model subscribes to the homogeneous unit principle. Many consider Donald McGavran to be the "father of the modern church growth movement" through his development of the homogeneous unit principle. McGavran defines a homogeneous unit as a "section of society in which all the members have something in common."[64] McGavran first introduced the homogeneous unit principle in the 1970 original version of *Understanding Church Growth*. The rationale behind the homogeneous unit principle is that people movements are an effective mode of evangelism. McGavran furthers his theory by explaining, "Men and women like to become Christians without crossing linguistic, racial, and class lines."[65] It is true that as human beings we generally tend to stay in our comfort zones. This tendency

---

[64] McGavran, Donald A. *Understanding Church Growth* (Grand Rapids, MI: Eerdmans, 1980), 136.

[65] Ibid. p. 100.

to be around people with whom we identify, whether it is by ethnicity, language, socioeconomic status, or even gender, is seen within the segregation of cities and churches across America. McGavran researched three questions:

1. What causes churches to grow outside of the common insights?
2. Why do some churches not grow, and what are the barriers or obstructions that prevent the natural growth of the body of Christ?
3. What are the reproducible principles behind church growth? McGavran believed that if there were enough studies conducted on growing churches that some of those principles could be reproducible.

While McGavran's questions were legitimate and he uncovered some useful insights, we believe the goal should be moving *past* similarities to bridge the gap. The Kingdom of God is about crossing barriers and uniting people through the cross of Christ. The Apostle Paul succinctly communicates this in 2 Corinthians 5:18-19, "All this is from God, who through Christ reconciled us to himself and gave us the ministry of reconciliation; that is, in Christ God was reconciling the world to himself, not counting their trespasses against them, and entrusting to us the message of reconciliation" (NIV).

When planting churches or revitalizing them, the homogeneous unit principle is often a reality. The planter or pastor is going to attract people who are like him or her. Homogeneity is more comfortable, but it falls short of God's intent for the coming Kingdom of God.

We certainly find this to be true in the story of our friend Sarah Heath, who is the pastor of First United Methodist

Church of Costa Mesa in Costa Mesa, California. Sarah sat down with us to tell the story of how her church has taken on a local dive mentality that has resulted in its growth to over four times what it was when she arrived.

She has discovered that vitality can grow out intentionally working towards developing a faith community where people don't look alike and even span generations. Sarah – an elder millennial pastor - has striven to create a church that is for everyone; not just for people who are her age or demographic.

> *"When I was in the process of exploring planting, the strategies at the time were centered around the idea that you needed to have a demographic in mind and shoot for it. Those responsible for raising up planters in our system might look at someone like me and think, 'Sarah, you need to plant a church geared toward young people'. While I understand that thinking, it just didn't feel like the right fit for me. It was too limiting and didn't reflect the Kingdom of God.*
>
> *There are plenty of boutique-y churches around that are only going for one generation. I began to recognize that the nuclear family is changing. These days, it seems people aren't around others who are different ages than them as much as they once were. The thing is, we can really benefit from the experiences and relationships that come from those who are older and younger than us."*

Sarah identifies the people who are "spiritual nomads" and those who have experienced spiritual deconstruction or a spiritual shift. She said that she is trying to reach outside the boundaries of Methodism (her tribe) to those who may not fully understand the liturgies and practices (methods) that people within the church understand.

Does that mean she has abandoned those liturgies and

sacred spaces for smoke machines and moving lights? Not at all. Instead, she has gone out of her way to strategically explain - in an artful way - the symbolism of the moments take place in worship.

> *One of the ways we have helped bridge generations is to craft worship in such a way that it is familiar to those who have been here for decades, but with explanations of what those rituals and practices mean. I have found that people are curious about the rituals associated with more traditional services, especially if they are coming out of non-denominational settings, or have experienced spiritual deconstruction. It's interesting how even when we are unsure what we believe practices can orient us toward the divine. You have to be intentional explaining the worship rituals to allow them to attach meaning to them.*

These practices haven't only benefited the younger people in her congregation, or those less familiar with church. Sarah had a congregant in her 90s say how she'd been in church her whole life and didn't understand the meaning behind the lighting of candles in worship until it was explained one Sunday.

When Sarah was appointed to Costa Mesa, she began - as every pastor does - making changes here and there. The mostly older legacy congregation pushed back at some of the changes she wanted to make where the building was concerned. She was very clear with them that her vision wasn't to create worship and space only for those who would come, but that those spaces and the worship that occurred within them was also for the people who were already there.

Sarah is a gifted artist, who loves to do reclamation work. She takes old things and makes them new so that they may take on purposes. Believing in the power of spaces to make relationships happen, she has taken many steps to remodel and rework the church to become more community centric.

When she first began the work of revitalization, a lot of folks were coming with kids, and there were no rooms for ready to receive them. Sarah's first project was to create a cry/play room that allowed new folks to have a space for their little ones. At first that was hard for legacy congregation, but once the sound of kids was heard echoing throughout the building – something that hadn't been heard in years – Sarah began to gain trust. In time, they ended up making a coffee bar/warming kitchen in part of the lobby, which has become a gathering space before and after worship. This is another way in which intentional space is fostering community at their church. Over time, Sarah continued to gain trust by making spaces that people could gather in.

> *We need to create space where people can encounter God and each other. The appeal of the local dive is that it's the place where everyone knows your name. With that in mind, one of the most dramatic changes I made, which came after a lot of intentional relational work with the existing congregation, was to rework the layout of the sanctuary to better facilitate community and connection.*
>
> *The pews were detached from the floor, and wheels were added that allow us to reconfigure the sanctuary. Worship is more in the round with seats facing the center of the room, rather than being in rows. I didn't propose removing the pews permanently (which the existing congregation would have hated and is often a selling point for weddings), so that eased the angst that might have otherwise been felt. We can always reset the space back to its original layout when we need to, which created great peace of mind for our long-time members.*

> *The seating and the way it's arranged now is intentional and is part of what I'm trying to bring to the worship experience. I don't see myself as the keeper of the knowledge, but more as a fellow journeyer with them. I absolutely share with them what I hear God saying as their pastor, but I want them to see each other and wrestle through their faith together. It's a lot harder to do that in rows.*

Sarah laid the groundwork for some of these changed by doing a series on Deconstructing Faith, using reclaimed items such as worn out/weathered front doors that were re-purposed into a bench and a communion table. Sarah recognizes sometimes the doors that got us into church need to be re-purposed in ways that help us sit, eat and be present with one another.

The worship and the space aren't the only thing that is intentionally intergenerational. Even their groups aren't age based. Sarah and the people at First United are thriving in a recipe that is oozing purpose and strategic action.

Reflection Questions:

If you're revitalizing an existing worship experience, are you building it in such a way that it isn't about both the legacy congregation and the one to come?

Are you intentionally creating opportunities for people of different generations to come together?

Are there opportunities to reclaim space in your church to better foster relationships?

The shift from homogeneity to local dive is not easy. It can actually be messy as people come together who don't speak the same cultural language, come from different generators, or possess a like-minded worldview. However, the shift is worth making as one sees glimpses of God's Kingdom coming to earth. We believe an important set of questions church planters and revitalizers (and Christians in general) need to ask include: *What type of people make us feel uncomfortable and why? What are our biases and prejudices? Who are "those" people in our mind?* We have seen instances where the moment we become honest with God and ourselves, we open the door of possibility to embodying a ministry of reconciliation as a reality.

Another con to the franchise model can be that, without intentionality, barriers to innovation can be erected. If you are on the ground as a leader in a franchise model church, it is difficult to implement new ideas and change. There are systems in place and supply chain issues. With complex moving parts, it's hard to pivot. In a franchise restaurant, a local owner can't simply convince upper management to accept a new product. In a local dive, freedom and the flexibility to experiment and implement ideas are natural.

This tension between ideation and franchise was seen in the 2017 movie, *Founder*, which tells the story of Ray Kroc and his creation of the McDonald's chain. Kroc entered a franchise agreement with Maurice "Mac" McDonald and Richard "Dick" McDonald, the McDonald brothers. As Kroc was experiencing financial woes and eventually found his way out by finding big money in the real estate of the McDonald's building, he broke several franchise rules. One memorable episode related to the cost and limitation of McDonald's milkshake production. Due to the cost of buying and refrigerating ice cream, along with the time it took to make the shakes, the milkshake was leading in profit loss among the business' products. One day, Kroc was introduced to a powdered milk-shake mix that would save the company money, but would reduce the overall quality that the McDonald's aimed for. Kroc, with growth and franchising in mind, saw dollar signs and took every step he could to circumvent the brother's authority, eventually buying his way out of the franchise contract. There was no way for Kroc to introduce innovative ideas at McDonald's.[66]

In 1962, Kroc bought McDonald's from the brothers and continued to expand. Although Kroc himself had to buy the entire business to get his own innovations approved, some franchise owners in the early days of McDonald's had more freedom to experiment.[67]

When McDonald's franchisee Lou Groen noticed a drop in sales on Fridays in his predominantly Roman Catholic neighborhood, he sought a way to bring in more customers. It was 1962, and McDonald's was a brand primarily serving hamburgers. Catholic customers couldn't consume hamburgers on Fridays in the spring, in observance of Lent. Groen created a fish sandwich. It required a more complicated preparation process than McDonald's was used to, so the company wasn't initially sold on offering it.

Meanwhile, Kroc had plans for what he called the Hula Burger—a slice of grilled pineapple and cheese on a bun. He made a deal with Groen that whichever sandwich sold the most on a Friday would be added to the permanent menu. Kroc was reportedly so confident in the Hula Burger that he made a side bet with employee Fred Turner that the burger would outsell the fish sandwich, and the loser would buy the

---

[66] Edelstein, David. "'Founder' Serves Up a Profile of the Man Behind McDonald's," *NPR*, , www.npr.org/2017/01/23/511215010/founder-serves-up-a-profile-of-the-man-behind-mcdonalds, January 23, 2017.

[67] "Ray Krock," Wikipedia.org. https://en.wikipedia.org/wiki/Ray_Kroc. Accessed December 18, 2019.

winner a new suit.

Turner got a new suit, and Groen got the Filet-O-Fish added to the permanent menu as a 29 cent item, and the first non-hamburger sandwich option.[68]

When a franchise makes allowances for the local context, real wins are possible. Groen knew what would work in his community. Kroc, with all of his experience and business acumen found he couldn't simply impose what may have suited his tastes.

Five years later the Big Mac was invented by Pittsburgh area franchisee Jim Dellgatti.[69] And five years after that Santa Barbara franchisee Herb Peterson and his assistant Donald Greadel invented the Egg McMuffin.[70]

Ironically, under Kroc's leadership, the experimentation and freedom he once sought from the brothers to try new things came to an end. In time, franchisees had to follow strict rules. Kroc mandated that, "The food was to be of a strictly fixed, standardized content and restaurants were not allowed to deviate from specifications in any way."[71]

Franchise churches must find a balance between maintaining consistent DNA, quality, and other standards, while allowing for innovation and menu tweaks.

---

[68] Dixon, Alex. "The History of McDonald's Filet-O-Fish," *QSR* https://www.qsrmagazine.com/news/history-filet-o-fish, March 6, 2017.

[69] "Big Mac," Wikipedia.org (Wikimedia Foundation), en.wikipedia.org/wiki/Big_Mac. Accessed December 18, 2019.

[70] "McMuffin," Wikipedia.org (Wikimedia Foundation), en.wikipedia.org/wiki/McMuffin. Accessed December 18, 2019.

[71] "Ray Kroc," Wikipedia.org. https://en.wikipedia.org/wiki/Ray_Kroc. Accessed December 18, 2019.

Reflection Question:

What level of freedom is the franchisor granting to the franchisee to change up the ministry menu?

Innovation is often a response to an issue or problem. Many times, executives are not aware of what people on the ground are encountering on a daily basis. If the people on the ground are simply viewed as employees and their feedback is not welcomed, they will grow resentful. A franchise model doesn't foster a spirit of innovation among everyone in the organization. Innovation seems reserved for a few at the top. Many people want to accomplish something bigger than themselves, but don't give themselves permission to dream—or others don't allow them the permission. Local dives have the freedom to be innovative when there is a problem to solve or a way to reach more customers. They aren't held back by the rules and regulations of a franchise.

When Roz began vocational ministry, he chose United Methodism because of its sound theology, emphasis on grace and sanctification, accountability, and structure. However, there are times when "we" (the denomination) get in our own way of opportunities and innovation. Craig Groeschel, who leads LifeChurch.tv, exemplifies this reality. LifeChurch is the third largest church in America with twenty-seven locations. Craig Groeschel was once a United Methodist. In fact,

> *Groeschel, who attended various United Methodist churches in Texas and Oklahoma growing up, did his undergraduate work at Oklahoma City University (a UMC school) and entered ministry as an associate pastor of First United Methodist Church in downtown Oklahoma City. When he wanted to plant a new UMC*

church, it wasn't an option for him because he was only ordained as a "deacon" and not an "elder."[72]

Groeschel explains his frustration and parting of ways with the Methodists:

When I was a UMC pastor, I was an un-ordained "local pastor" for three years, spent four years in seminary (while serving full-time at a church) and had two more years before I'd become fully ordained as an elder. While I appreciate the education and accountability, many younger leaders want to be "in the game" more than they want to leap through lots of denominational hurdles. Today's emerging Christian leaders are eager to make a difference – now. Our burden to start a church became greater than our loyalty to a denomination. We left the UMC on good terms with fond memories and many great relationships.[73]

Groeschel left the United Methodist Church in 1996 and shortly after planted LifeChurch. The irony is that LifeChurch partners with many churches and denominations, including the United Methodist Church, who use LifeChurch's teaching and sermon resources without charge. Perhaps Groeschel has been able to make a greater impact on the franchise from outside it than within it. Nonetheless, this demonstrates the limits of a structure without give.[74]

Another advantage to a local dive is its simple structure.

---

[72] Barrick, Audrey. "Megachurch Pastor Offers Advice for United Methodists," *The Christian Post*, www.christianpost.com/news/megachurch-pastor-offers-advice-for-united-methodists-43986/, February 26, 2010

[73] Ibid.

[74] Ibid.

Multi-site churches and megachurches, like franchises, can become so complex that they aren't nimble enough to make timely decisions. Even innovative, vibrant franchises with capable leaders can struggle to turn the rudder quickly enough because of boards, hierarchy, and budget constraints. By the time a decision is made, an opportunity has already passed by.

In the business world, this is called "opportunity cost." It can simply be defined as, "the price of the next best thing you could have done had you not made your first choice."[75] We're not suggesting local dives (in business and in the church) automatically get this right. Because of their small size, they have the advantage of positioning themselves in a way that most franchises and larger churches cannot.

So, what happens when a franchise or a megachurch coasts on past victories and fails to innovate? Think: Blockbuster! In 2000, Reed Hastings, the owner of a small, grassroots company called Netflix reached out to Blockbuster CEO John Antioco to meet about a potential partnership that would allow Netflix to be promoted in stores with the return promise that Netflix would promote the Blockbuster brand online. The meeting was an epic failure resulting in Hastings walking out of the room in embarrassment.

Fast-forward to present day, Netflix is worth more than ten times Blockbuster's peak value, and now there are empty Blockbuster buildings standing on town corners all over the U.S. Another reason for the downfall of Blockbuster was that much of their revenue was derived from late fee charges their customers racked up when returning a video late. Netflix had no major capital building expenses, they could charge cheaper rates for subscriptions, and their customers would not fall

---

[75] Kennon, Joshua. "A Guide to Understanding the Basics of Opportunity Cost," *The Balance*, www.thebalance.com/what-is-opportunity-cost-357200., February 27, 2018.

victim to late fees.[76] What companies like Netflix, Redbox, Uber, and others have carried out is known as "disruptive innovation," which is "a term of art coined by Clayton Christensen, describes a process by which a product or service takes root initially in simple applications at the bottom of a market and then relentlessly moves up market, eventually displacing established competitors."[77]

Netflix wasn't an overnight success. It faced challenges. Without physical locations it was hard for people to grasp the idea of an online video streaming service. However, people adapt to change or subscribe to a product in different ways. A helpful way to grasp this is the "diffusions of innovation" theory developed by E.M. Rogers in 1962. Rogers broke down his theory into five basic adopter categories:

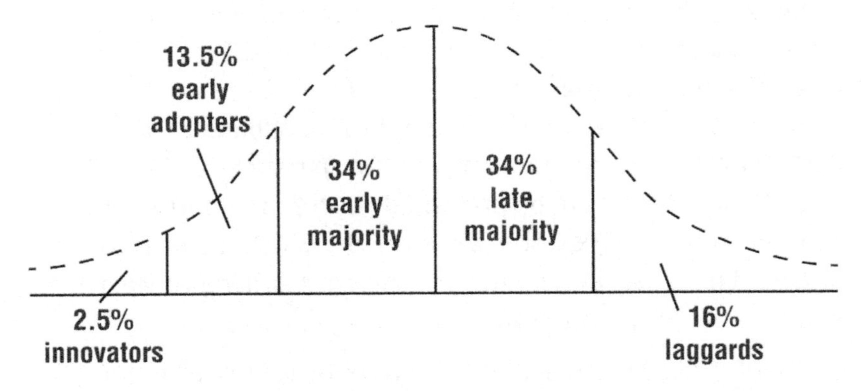

1. **Innovators** - These are people who want to be the first to try the innovation. They are venturesome and interested in new ideas. These people are very willing to take risks, and

[76] Satell, Greg. "A Look Back at Why Blockbuster Really Failed and Why It Didn't Have To," *Forbes Magazine*, www.forbes.com/sites/gregsatell/2014/09/05/a-look-back-at-why-blockbuster-really-failed-and-why-it-didnt-have-to/, September 21, 2014.

[77] "Disruptive Innovation," *Clayton Christensen*, www.claytonchristensen.com/key-concepts/, October 23, 2012.

are often the first to develop new ideas. Very little, if anything, needs to be done to appeal to this population.

2. **Early Adopters** - These are people who represent opinion leaders. They enjoy leadership roles, and embrace change opportunities. They are already aware of the need to change and so are very comfortable adopting new ideas. Strategies to appeal to this population include how-to manuals and information sheets on implementation. They do not need information to convince them to change.

3. **Early Majority** - These people are rarely leaders, but they do adopt new ideas before the average person. That said, they typically need to see evidence that the innovation works before they are willing to adopt it. Strategies to appeal to this population include success stories and evidence of the innovation's effectiveness.

4. **Late Majority** - These people are skeptical of change, and will only adopt an innovation after it has been tried by the majority. Strategies to appeal to this population include information on how many other people have tried the innovation and have adopted it successfully.

5. **Laggards** - These people are bound by tradition and very conservative. They are very skeptical of change and are the hardest group to bring on board. Strategies to appeal to this population include statistics, fear appeals, and pressure from people in the other adopter groups.[78]

---

[78] LaMorte, Wayne W. "Diffusion of Innovation Theory," *The Theory of Planned Behavior*, Boston University School of Public Health, sphweb.bumc.bu.edu/otlt/MPH-Modules/SB/BehavioralChangeTheories/BehavioralChangeTheories4.html, April 28, 2016.

Rogers contends that on the spectrum, the bulk of people are early and late majority adopters (34% each), while 2.5% are innovators, 13.5% are early adopters, and 16% are laggards. Of course, there are many variables at play, but Netflix and other disruptors in their fields had the freedom to experiment and were nimble enough to make timely decisions. Netflix bridged the gap between brick-and-mortar DVD stores by doing a combination of DVD by mail and streaming. In the early days, network speeds and limited data services made the streaming option less useful to subscribers. There were fewer titles available, and they hadn't begun to produce original content yet.

As speeds improved, data became cheaper, and DVDs became less common, many customers shifted towards streaming and away from physical media. In fact, the vast majority of Netflix subscribers no longer subscribe to the DVD option.

In 2019, Netflix found its long reign at the top of the streaming kingdom challenged. In the fall of that year, Apple+ and Disney+ joined the ranks of HBO, Amazon Prime Video, Hulu, and others producing original content that is competing at a high level. These late adopters pose a very real threat to Netflix and it will have to reinvent itself if it is to survive into the future.

Reflection Questions:

How can structures and systems be modified/adjusted to maximize effectiveness for both parties?

How can you proactively establish practices that keep what you're offering fresh?

What these disruptor companies show is that they are in touch with felt needs of people. Local dives and churches have the opportunity to do this in any given community, regardless of size, through incarnational ministry.

In Roz's first few years of doing urban ministry, he learned that the most impactful way to reach people was living among them, which meant moving into the neighborhood, shopping at the same grocery stores and shops, working out at the same gyms, and eating at the same restaurants. He fully immersed himself in the community. The example of incarnational ministry is Jesus. We love the way Eugene Peterson puts it so eloquently when he paraphrase's John1:14a, "The Word became flesh and blood, and moved into the neighborhood."[79]

The incarnation was an indescribable and powerful collision between God and humanity. Jesus became God with us, living in our world. But what does the incarnation have to do with church planting? Everything! Jesus leaves us the example of how to live with people. The Son of God was born as a baby, circumcised on the eighth day, and spoke the language of his people. Jesus fully immersed himself not only in the Jewish culture, but also in the human race.

Megachurches with a franchise satellite may have difficulty being incarnational to all of their communities unless they can get beyond being homogeneous. It is imperative that churches planting new faith communities embrace the value of the local dive, its context, people, and preferred flavors. Although communities and demographics can appear similar on the surface, no two are exactly alike. They each have their intricacies and quirks.

The United Methodist Church of the Resurrection near

---

[79] Peterson, Eugene H. "John 1:14a," *The Message: the Bible in Contemporary Language* (Colorado Springs, CO: NavPress, 2017), 1916.

Kansas City has done a masterful job adapting their menus to the local context through well-chosen campus pastors, congruent ambiance at its satellite campuses, and intentional contextual ministry. What works in Leawood (the home church) has to be served up differently for the downtown Kansas City location.

For a local dive to thrive and tensions to be held at bay, the relationships established between the main campus and its offspring have to be carefully orchestrated. An important factor in successful partnering between local dives and franchises is the type of control each multi-site faith community has. This can determine its ability to be incarnational and contextual.

ELEVATION CHURCH, CHARLOTTE, NC

Two examples of this are Elevation Church and North Point Church, both very successful multi-site megachurches. Elevation Church was founded in 2006 and is based in St. Matthews, North Carolina. It is pastored by Steven Furtick, has seventeen campuses – nine in the Charlotte area – and locations in Raleigh, Winston-Salem, Roanoke, Melbourne, and the Greater Toronto Area. Without a doubt, God has worked through Stephen Furtick and Elevation Church.[80] Their satellite model is an example of a thriving franchise.

[80] "Locations, Elevation Church," www.elevationchurch.org/locations/. Accessed December 18, 2019.

NORTHPOINT COMMUNITY CHURCH, ALPHARETTA, GA

Each location shares the same elements and décor. The worship teams sing the same songs, share the same order of worship and environment. The preaching is the same across sites. Each site has a campus pastor who reinforces the DNA and helps with pastoral leadership. They do not deviate from the script, and there is no contextualization. Elevation's model is a straightforward example of a franchise. In this model, being situated in similar/like-minded communities with similar demographics is extremely important. There are numerous other stories of churches that have tried to replicate their DNA to the tiniest detail in a new community, only to never have those plants take root.

But not all megachurch satellite strategies are the same. North Point Community Church, under the leadership of Andy Stanley, has six campuses and worships with around 36,000 people on a weekly basis. North Point's strategy is more of a hybrid approach. Without a doubt, Andy Stanley is the leader, but each pastor at the satellite locations is called the lead pastor instead of the campus pastor because it makes sense to unchurched people. This also allows room for each location to preach its own sermon series. For example, in the summer of 2018, four out of the six campuses preached their own sermon series. There seems to be a delicate balance between a "central team" who controls everything from one location, and a local team who is indigenous and on the ground at their respective locations. There is no one definition of autonomy at North Point. There are certain aspects that are centralized like preschool, safety precautions, and curriculum. But there is a lot of room for autonomy when it comes to outreach and even designing the worship service. The key for North Point to be more decentralized than other megachurches is the investment that Andy Stanley makes in his local leaders. North Point is quick to point out that when things are too controlled and centralized, they are not allowing great leaders to lead, thereby making it difficult to attract leaders at the local level.[81] For locations in the surrounding areas that want to partner with North Point, there is a strategic partnership track available through which churches can become affiliates, take advantage of North Point's resources, curriculum, and coaching, without giving up their autonomy. This has helped North Point spread its influence nationwide.[82]

This past year two megachurches have made the conscious decision to "multi-site" and contextualize in their own way. Pastor Matt Chandler of The Village Church has seven campuses across the Dallas Fort Worth area. The church has decided to allow all of its campuses to become independent so that the focus is on the local level and church planting. This process is planned to be strategically completed by 2022, as "the churches will roll out new names, original preaching, and more 'contextualized' ministry programs."[83] Rolling out autonomous churches has also been a strategy to help in successful succession planning at Redeemer Presbyterian in New York. As Tim Keller, the founding pastor for twenty-eight

---

[81] Rohane, Kyle. "Does Your Church Have the Right Model?" *Christianity Today* , www.christianitytoday.com/pastors/2017/june-web-exclusives/does-your-church-have-right-model.html, June 2017.

[82] "Explore Partnership, North Point Partners," www.northpointpartners.org/partnership. Accessed December 18, 2019.

[83] Shellnutt, Kate et al., "Matt Chandler's Village Church Ends Multi-site Era," *Christianity Today*, www.christianitytoday.com/news/2017/september/matt-chandler-village-church-end-multisite-campuses-dfw.html, September 28, 2017.

years was about to retire, the church decided to become three separate autonomous churches for its missional strategy to impact New York City.[84]

There is an intentionality and urgency from leaders to return to the local dive. Smaller churches, mid-size, and even megachurches are starting to recognize that they must create engagement on the local level as the United States becomes an even more post-Christian culture. As leaders in the local church, no matter our function or role, we have the unique opportunity to encourage a local presence in our communities if the church is going to be relatable to the next generation.

Reflection Questions:

How is your franchisor pastor pouring into and mentoring your local dive pastors?

What is your long-term plan for how the local dive(s) will relate to the franchise in the future?

[84] Shellnutt, Kate et al., "Tim Keller Stepping Down as Redeemer Senior Pastor," *Christianity Today*, www.christianitytoday.com/news/2017/february/tim-keller-stepping-down-nyc-redeemer-senior-pastor.html, February 26, 2017.

CHAPTER 3
MENU PLANNING
THE COVENANT AGREEMENT

When it comes to the success of a place like Lily's Bistro (one of our favorite local dives), menu planning is essential. If you're going to change your menu up all the time, you have to know what you're going to cook, when you're going to cook it, and how the meals will be prepared.

In this chapter, we want to drill down into some of the specifics that must be considered when planning for your local dive.

One of the foundational pieces that must be considered when establishing a winning relationship between something that exists and something new is determining how uniform, interdependent, or autonomous the relationship will be on a number of aspects of ministries.

This applies to everything from starting a new faith community to starting a new service and/or revitalizing something that already exists.

Failure to properly plan ahead and consider how uniform, interdependent or anonymous the relationship will be, can lead to strife, anguish and tension between what exists and what is new.

Our friend Pastor Rachel Gilmore learned this the hard way when she became the planting pastor at The Gathering - a church within a church in Virginia Beach, Virginia. Courthouse Community United Methodist Church had a desire to plant a new church with the aim of reaching more young people. Prior to hiring Rachel, a team of leaders developed an extensive document outlining what they wanted the new church to look like. The selected their target demographic and set out to put the plan in motion.

With very good intentions, there were a number of important factors they hadn't considered in their initial pre-work. Chief among them was the fact that they did all of visioning prior to finding their leader. This makes a shared understanding of vision and ministry nearly impossible to achieve.

Second, their named target audience was college age young people in a non-college town 40 minutes from the closest major campus. Nonetheless they decided to move forward and the service began meeting in a separate space within the existing building. The 11AM worship time included brunch and an atmosphere friendly to new people.

Rachel describes the target audience to us like this:

> *We were trying to reach four main groups: 1.) young adult married couples 2.) Young adult unmarried people and 3.) Families with young children and 4.) College age kids. We were doing our best to connect with those folks and we were having some success.*
>
> *The deck was stacked against us in a sense, because our parent congregation provided no childcare or children's worship on Sunday mornings as the number of young families continued to grow. In fact, when folks from the legacy congregation saw young families come in with kids, they would attempt divert them toward the main service. Without malicious intent, they sort of looked at us as competition.*

Rachel began building relationships in the community and grew the service to about forty people. Things became more and more tense as time went on between The Gathering and Courthouse Community. Initially, money given in the offering at the new service could not be used by The Gathering, but instead were taken and added to the coffers of the existing congregation. The expectation on their end was that grant money should fund the burgeoning congregation. This decision only served to add to the growing rift.

When tensions grew to the point where the discomfort between the two parties was no longer tenable, the planting congregation asked The Gathering to leave. In a Paul and Barnabas type moment, the planting congregation sent the new congregation forth to do their own thing. Both parties recognized that the churches had different visions and it would be best to release one another to do their own respective ministries.

Rachel reflected back on this journey:

When I took this position, I initially struggled with my call. Was I meant to be a planter? I was fresh out of seminary, a 27-year-old mother, planting a college age ministry in a non-college town. Could this really be right for me?

When I went to planting boot camp I'd sometimes hear things like, 'women don't usually plant. And young mother's never plant churches.' Those words were ringing in my ears.

I distinctly remember a day when I was actively seeking God's voice asking if this is where I was supposed to be. In the matter of 45 minutes, I had three major confirmations: a phone call, email and text all came over that were about as clear as a bell that God was in this. Despite the adversity I faced in the initial partnership, I knew this is what I was supposed to be doing.

After we were asked to move, the search began for a new home. Turns out the local performing arts theater made for the perfect space for us and our goals of reaching spiritual nomads.

On that first Sunday, The Gathering launched with about 125 people. Only one day before public launch, Rachel learned that she was pregnant. Not only would she be launching a new church, but she'd be launching a new child into the world.

Things at the performing arts center continued to grow

and Rachel and her team saw a new opportunity to have an impact on the community. With the exorbitant cost of daycare in their area, and with church buildings sitting on underutilized space, The Gathering launched The Gathering Academic Preschool.

One local United Methodist church partnered with The Gathering allowing the school to use rooms that were otherwise sitting idle during the week. The aim of the school is to provide affordable childcare, while being committed to academic excellence, in a loving and warm Christian environment. It also provides scholarships to those who cannot afford such care. Years later, a second location was opened at another United Methodist Church.

In the time that Gathering Academic Preschools have been in operation, they have offered up to 95% scholarships to numerous families, giving away over a quarter of a million dollars in education and care.

At the same time the preschool was growing, The Gathering was bursting at the seams and was in need of a new space to worship. The team began praying that God would lead them to a new venue.

They found and renovated a warehouse space and experienced a 20% growth spurt after opening. In just two short years, and even more growth, they had maxed out that space and had to begin dreaming big again.

> *We were worshiping 200-250 people weekly with over 50 kids involved in Sunday morning services. While better than the performing arts center, we began to hit the limits of what we could do in the warehouse. We began praying and dreaming about what God might do next at The Gathering. An opportunity to merge with Scott Memorial United Methodist Church – a church that shares a lot of the same vision and DNA as us – arose*

and the two became one. On our first Sunday together, we saw hundreds of people worship in a space that was so much better than what we had before. It was a total win for both communities.

The Gathering continues to experience much success with numerous ministries to the homeless and marginalized in the area. Rachel has since moved into a new role as director of recruiting, assessing and training for church planting at Path 1 Church/New Church Starts.

One cannot deny God worked in the midst of the chaos of the initial launch and separation, but not every story turns out this way.

Reflection Questions:

If you're starting a new service/site/ministry are you visioning with the new leader? If not can you leave room for them to make it their own?

What intentional steps will you take to avoid a competitive spirit to emerge between the existing ministry and the new one?

Rachel's story helps us to see that shared understandings are a must. We've created a tool to help you navigate those early conversations to insure the most favorable outcome possible.

We think of it as the Franchise to Local Dive Continuum. On one end you have uniform, on the other end you have autonomous. In the middle is interdependence.

uniform interdependent autonomous

FRANCHISE LOCAL DIVE

Assessing where your church is on the continuum on several key aspects of ministry can save much heartache and conflict. It can also prevent your new ministry from fizzling in record time.

The left extreme of the continuum is where things are more local franchise-esque. In this understanding, uniformity is valued over autonomy. Uniformity dictates that very few things look and feel different from the established ministry. Governing structure, branding concerns, student and family ministries, worship series, music, preaching, and more, may all look nearly identical. A more franchise-oriented ministry will live more on the left end of the continuum.

On the opposite extreme of the continuum things are more local dive-esque. The new thing (faith community, service, campus) may have a completely different name, logo and branding, worship series and preaching style, music, student ministry, and more. A more local dive-oriented ministry will favor the right end of the continuum.

We're not suggesting that one is bad and the other is good, but failure to consider what expectations are between the planting entity and the planter can lead to failure for both parties.

As Jason's former ministry partner Len Wilson used to say (quoting his father, U.S. Army Colonel H. Wayne Wilson), "Mistakes made in the initial deployment cannot be overcome."

Regardless of what you're building (whether it be more of a franchise or a local dive in nature), you may find that some aspects of ministry need to be uniform, while others may be more autonomous. Ideally, some aspects of ministry would live in the interdependence zone where both parties can learn from one another.

Roz has two beautiful daughters, Lily and Gabriella. He shares that one of his biggest learnings was that his and his wife Callie's strategy had to change when they went from one child to two. The same is true for starting a new campus, service, or ministry. You can't just operate in the same way you always have when there is a second operation to consider.

Jason adds that while it's easy to think that parents are offering all of the wisdom and learning opportunities to their children, the children can teach the parents new things if they're receptive to learning from them. There is a very real possibility of mutual growth and interdependence even in these familial relationships.

We believe that a formal, written covenant agreement or letter of understanding should be drafted by all parties participating from the beginning of the new endeavor. The agreement should include several areas of ministries for consideration, but before we get to those, we think it's important to discuss the idea of determining a target audience.

Those two words – target audience – often feel like dirty words in the church. Choosing your target completely determines the strategies you'll take to achieve success. If you're looking to reach middle age parents with young kids, your ministry will look very different than it will if you're looking to minister to millennials. If you're trying to create a worship experience that is meaningful to boomers, it might look very different than a ministry geared to those in recovery.

One might be concerned that picking a target might exclude those outside of the stated target. This notion isn't true. For instance, Nike – a shoe and apparel company – has determined that its primary target is athletes. There are plenty of people who sport the swoosh on their shoes, shirts, hats, and other items who are far from being identified as athletes.

Determining your target might also help you determine where you are on the continuum. If your target is similar to the church you've already established – you want to go multi-site and open a new campus that is in a similar demographic to the one you're in – you might have more of a uniform feel.

If your target audience looks very different, you may find yourself on the more autonomous end of the continuum.

Here are the non-negotiables that we believe should be worked out in written form using the continuum as a guide for how uniform, interdependent, and autonomous several aspects of ministries should be:

Letter of intent/covenant agreement

1. Governing Structure

It's very easy to forget that starting something new requires new leadership. It would likely be more convenient to start a new thing with an existing board, but the new thing (campus, service, etc.) should also have representation amongst the board. Having advocates present to express the needs of the new thing is valuable for the success of the new endeavor. It is also good for accountability to include leaders from the new thing on the board as they have a much more up close and personal look at what's taking place on the ground.

A couple of key questions might be helpful to wrestle with when it comes to the board:

What percentage of the board should be made up of the new campus, service, or ministry? Does the new thing have its own board that interfaces and meets with the existing one?

The answers to those questions should be wrestled through and included in the covenant agreement. The essential functions of many church boards include: trustees, finance, human resources (or SPRC - Staff Parish Relations Committee in our United Methodist tribe).

In the United Methodist world that Roz and Jason come from, the head of nominations for these board positions is the pastor.

It is imperative to get the right leaders in place to represent the new thing as well as having the right people in place to represent the existing thing.

When it comes to selecting board members, consider these four factors.

- **Service**

Are they serving in the church outside of the role of being a board member? People who are already serving express a passion and an "all-in spirit" that qualifies them for a seat at the table. We recommend strongly encouraging some kind of additional service outside of being on the board. This gives a deeper understanding of what's happening within the church.

- **Giving**

Are your board members contributing to the church? More importantly, are they tithing? Potential board members who are not tithing should not be considered.

Tithing and stewardship are among the primary tenants of our faith. Leadership starts at the top, and board members should model and set the standard for the church.

- **Expertise**

When recruiting board members, ask what knowledge, wisdom, skills, or expertise they bring to the table. Do they work in HR at their company? Are they in finance? Are they a savvy businessperson? Church boards can easily be made up of those who hold seniority in the church, and while beloved members are cherished, they may bring nothing of leadership value to the team.

- **Good Interview Skills**

Church boards can make or break a church and a new movement. They have influence over many areas in the church and they will be making key decisions that affect your local dive. We believe that board members should apply and be interviewed in the same way that a high-level leader at a company would be.

2. Student Ministry

Growing something new requires different learning opportunities for different age groups. If you're starting a new worship experience, what will take place with families with young children? If you're starting a new campus or multi-site ministry, how will you minister to students at the new location(s)?

As you begin to process how these concerns are going to be addressed on the continuum, there are several factors to think through.

- **Curriculum**

Will the new thing be using the same curriculum as the existing thing? Will resources be shared between the two? How are these items budgeted for? Is there an expectation that there will be a uniform approach or an autonomous one?

- **Child Check-in**

Every church, no matter the size should have a formal child check-in procedure. These range from sophisticated digital systems, to simply sheets of paper on clipboards. We won't go into the many reasons your church should have a formal check-in, but if you don't have one, start there.

Many churches who are healthy enough to start a new thing likely have a check-in already in place. If there is a system already ready to go, will the new thing be using the same system, or a different one? How will the attendance of those children be tracked? Are they lumped into the same system and numbers of the existing entity, or will they be kept separate?

- **Staffing & Accountability**

Will the new thing have its own leader, or will the leader from the existing entity be covering the new thing as well? If creating a local dive at your church means starting a new worship experience that is different than what currently exists now, using the same staff person for both is very doable.

If your local dive means starting a new faith community, service, or multi-site ministry in a location that is new, it's nearly impossible to use the same leader/staff person in both locations.

Heaping too much on the shoulders of an existing staff member can lead to burnout, frustration, and may prevent success in both settings. Staffing for the new ministry should be carefully considered.

If hiring a new student ministry leader for the new thing, accountability is also an important consideration. Will the new leader report to the student ministry leader of the existing ministry, or will they be a peer to that person? If there will be a new hire for this role, what is the ideal timeline for this to happen? Will the new person report directly to the planting pastor or to the existing ministry staff?

We've seen the perils of confused accountability wreak havoc on churches who don't work these things out ahead of time. If the student/family ministry leader of the new thing doesn't report to the pastor of the new thing, but instead reports to the student ministries leader at the existing ministry, tensions can arise when requests are made and not followed.

It can work, but teams must be strategic about how decisions are going to be made and carried out. If the student ministry person from the existing ministry is over the person at the new ministry, it is imperative that they spend time with the new ministry so they can understand what's happening on the ground. Leading a second campus from a planting campus without seeing it action can also cause unneeded chaos.

- **Location of the ministry**

If your local dive will involve a second location like a school, movie theater, or a space that is only temporarily available to you, where is the student ministry going to take place? Will the existing ministry be hosting youth activities? Are there monies set aside to host youth/student events in a dedicated space?

Roz's church meets in a movie theater. While there are options for kids on Sunday mornings, the bulk of his student activities take place at a partnering church nearby the theater.

3. Music

Music is an invaluable aspect of local dive ministry. Finding the right sound for the music, talent to lead it, instrumentation and so on are monumental in launching well.

The covenant agreement should establish the target audience as defined earlier. That target will drive the music style. Get specific in the covenant about the expectations about the kinds of music that will be offered. This is one area where autonomy will likely win the day, and rightly so. If you're starting something new, new music (not uniform music) will be required.

With the style determined, choosing a leader is the next decision to make. If you're working to establish a new worship service, or a campus with a different flare from what exists, be sure to choose a leader that is in love with the style of music you intend to use in the new thing.

In Jason's two decades of coaching, he's encountered numerous churches who have made the traditional worship leader, the leader of the "contemporary" service. More often than not, these leaders are classically trained and have no real love for worship outside of this style. It's like asking a pastry chef to become a barbecue master. Both are cooks, but the flavors are very different.

Accountability also matters here. If you're going to hire a music director for your new thing, it makes much more sense to make them a peer to the existing music leader, rather than putting them under this person. Jason has witnessed at two different churches he coaches the tensions of having a non-traditional leader being directed or supervised by a traditional worship leader.

A pastry chef may know very little about how to run a grill. In the same way, an organist or choir director may know very little about music styles led by a band.

Another consideration that should be made is whether or not to pay band members. What is the standard that presently exists with the planting church/service? If excellence is to be offered in both settings, similar standards may need to be applied.

4. Teaching/Preaching

- **Series**

There is great potential for preaching and teaching to create rifts between the new and old thing if mutual understandings aren't arrived at prior to launch. Working out how uniform, interdependent, or autonomous the relationship will be is essential to its success.

Will the same series be preached at both the planting entity and the new entity? Is there freedom to veer from the plan on occasion? Will there be an interdependence where series concepts are originated by both parties? What will collaboration look like when developing series?

When there are different understandings of expectations around these questions, resentments can form, especially when series ideas are rejected or the new thing does its own series.

A church Jason was coaching experienced some of these tensions when it didn't carry out the series developed at the planting campus. Because these conversations weren't had ahead of time, the plant was moving in the direction it felt was best, while the planting congregation had some degree of frustration that the DNA it was providing would get lost without the series it was developing. Neither party was wrong as expectations were never set in the beginning.

As mentioned earlier, some churches take a "one church, two (or more) locations" mentality, and the expectation is that everything is going to look the same with series/preaching. Other churches share series where there is congruence with two or more different congregations, and others allow each location to respectively do its own thing.

- **Attire**

Another item that should be considered where preaching/teaching is concerned is what kind of attire will be worn by the leader. In some settings this could be a bigger consideration than one might think.

If a church that is currently living in a more traditional style of worship is looking to create a non-traditional expression of worship, clothing is a part of the shift that must be thought through. For some worshipers looking for a new flavor, attire will affect how they receive the meal.

Robes, stoles, and vestments fit well in a liturgical setting, but in a non-traditional setting feel out of place. At one church Jason coached, the pastor felt it necessary to stay dressed in the same attire as the traditional service with all of the aforementioned items on for the "contemporary" service. When asked about that choice, the pastor said he felt like some would revolt if he were to stand on the chancel without those things on. The pastor felt that the potential disconnect wasn't worth the fight with leadership that might ensue.

This is where the covenant agreement up front could have outlined putting the conflict in the pre-launch conversation and making for a more indigenous clothing choice for the non-traditional setting.

Of course, not all pastors wear these kinds of things in worship. Going from formal to informal attire to match the feel of the worship style (and its setting) should be considered by the leader.

- **Media**

One final consideration that should be made in regards to preaching is that of who will be producing media for the sermon. We're just going to assume that if you're doing something new, it'll involve screens. If your old thing involves screens and media is being produced for sermons (graphics, illustrations, points, and scripture), it is important to work out ahead of time how these things are being supported.

In many churches who are using media, there is someone already assigned (usually paid) to create sermon graphics. When the new thing begins, whether it be a new service, or a new location, how are those same functions going to be handled?

Will the same person who does media for the planting congregation be doing it for both locations? If the preacher at the new location is doing a different series, how will those graphics be handled? What level of accountability does the media producer have to the leader at the new endeavor?

5. Communications

Closely related to the last point around preaching and teaching, branding and communications must also be worked out in your covenant agreement.

Without intentionality, the local dive can end up getting short changed where communications and branding are concerned.

- **Branding, logo, design standards**

From website and social media, to graphics and print support, how you're communicating with the world about your local dive matters.

Will the local dive have its own logo? Will the fonts, color scheme, and design language used be the same or different than the existing brand? When there is not intentionality around branding for your local dive, it can be very confusing to the outsider. Significant time should be spent on this decision when writing your covenant agreement.

Jason was recently asked to secretly worship at a church plant meeting under a different name than its planting church, in its own building. Upon entering the parking lot, Jason encountered a well-crafted sign with the name of the church plant on it. On the sign was a very nicely designed logo. There was (appropriately) no mention of the parent church on the sign. If Jason hadn't been there to consult, he wouldn't have known it was a church plant. That is, until he was handed the printed bulletin when he entered the sanctuary.

The bulletin had the planting church's lead pastor listed above the campus pastor, and the logo from the planting church was present on this print piece. The plant's logo was nowhere to be found.

When Jason visited the website of the plant listed on the bulletin, he was taken to the planting congregation's website. There was no sign of the plant's logo, and the connection between the two congregations was confusing and hard to find information on. If you're trying to share one website for your established ministry and your new one, be careful to create clear distinction between the two entities.

Jason was recently told that the two congregations made the difficult decision to close this plant. It seems that there were many items that the planting congregation and the planting team didn't work out ahead of time and in the end, expectations were too far apart. One entity saw what was being done as uniform, the other autonomous. They lived in almost constant tension because these things weren't worked through in the pre-launch phase.

- **Print**

Finally, as you consider the new thing, keep in mind that print pieces also play an important role in communications. Quality standards matter just as much in the thing being established as they do in the established thing.

Will your new thing have separate business cards? Do you use lanyards for ministry workers? Do they have their own look and feel? How about bulletins, print pieces, etc.?

Another secret worshiper consultation took Jason to a church near Cleveland, Ohio. The church offers both traditional worship and non-traditional worship. The congregation is working hard to bring equal attention to both styles of worship. Print, however, (at the time) wasn't considered.

When Jason attended the traditional worship experience (the first service), a carefully designed insert was included with the bulletin that went into great detail about the many elements taking place in worship. For each moment in worship, there were names of leaders listed. There was an outline and a place to take notes.

When Jason returned for the non-traditional service, he discovered when he sat down that there was no insert. He believed maybe he'd gotten one where the insert was unintentionally omitted. He soon learned that none of the bulletins included an insert because inserts weren't made for this service. This resulted in not knowing any of the players in worship and having no way to really follow along with what was happening throughout.

As does sometimes happen, the new expression of worship can get the short end of the stick. The congregation can give the majority of its attention, resources, and efforts to the existing thing without really realizing it. The continuum is your friend. Use it!

Reflection Questions:

What are some of the non-negotiables that your local dive must include in its recipe?

As you write your covenant agreement, how much is to be uniform, interdependent, and autonomous in the areas of governing structure, student ministry, music, hospitality, teaching/preaching, and communications?

A winning recipe is within your grasp. In the next chapter, we'll explore how to move past pre-packaged, predictable cuisine, to farm fresh, authentic ingredients.

CHAPTER 4

NEW POSSIBILITIES

When it comes to fine (or even not so fine) dining, ingredients are everything. Even fast food giant McDonald's has come to this realization in recent years, stepping up its game and boasting, "Fresh beef, cooked when you order." What a novel idea.

Specialty burger franchises like Smashburger, Shake Shack, and Five Guys Burgers and Fries are taking a bite out of the fast food chain's profits in recent years.

> *McDonald's, the reigning market leader for casual dining, saw a sales drop of 2.4 percent and a 15 percent drop in net income in 2014, the first decline in those figures in thirty-three years. The study credits changed consumer tastes, in particular Smashburger›s popularity, because of a customer perception that Smashburger›s food is of higher quality and more customizable.*[85]

Many restaurants are presently smack dab in the middle of the plant-based meat craze. Everyone from Burger King with it's Impossible Whopper, to Dunkin Donuts with its non-meat sausage biscuit are getting in on the action. America's beef producers are holding their collective breath waiting to see if this phase sticks.

Hungry, health-conscious consumers are taking notice and have begun rejecting the chemical ingredients in so many of our convenience foods. Additives may allow food to be predictable, preserved, and pre-made, but they also make food less palatable and less healthy.

Similarly, church attendees have begun to feel the staleness

[85] "Smashburger" Wikipedia.org. https://en.wikipedia.org/wiki/Smashburger. Accessed December 18, 2019.

of the franchise model in the tired church practices, outdated music, lack of innovation in worship present throughout ministry.

Eating fresh for a local church means focusing on authentic ingredients and tailoring recipes to attendees' communities of origin. It's a continual battle to keep things fresh.

As a secret worshiper consultant and worship coach, Jason evaluates and re-imagines contemporary worship for those looking to revitalize their faith communities. He finds that few of the worship experiences that church communities call "contemporary" are truly contemporary.

At an event where Jason was speaking years ago, author and speaker Tony Campolo wisely proclaimed to the audience that the root of the word "contemporary" is "temporary." In other words, to keep worship fresh, it must continually change. We might argue that "contempt" would be a more accurate root word to describe some of the worship expressions we categorize as contemporary. Worship experiences with the local dive mentality need to be fresh to work for today's culture.

Even churches that are doing worship that is truly contemporary have to work hard to keep it fresh. The way to keep a winning recipe winning is to continue to tweak and improve it. It's easy to become attached to established, successful models to the point that they become stale without the church leadership realizing it.

EMBRACE CHURCH, SIOUX FALLS, SD

One of our friends, Adam Weber, has been a shining example of keeping things fresh at his church plant, called Embrace. Adam graciously shared with us the lessons he has learned at one of the fastest growing churches in the United Methodist denomination. He and his team are working hard to keep ingredients fresh in the way they do worship across their four campuses.

Adam began by admitting that Embrace started off as more of a classic franchise model, and over time it has become more of a local dive. Adam says, "When we first launched, we tightly controlled everything. All of the preaching mostly was me on video or carefully selected guest speakers. We worked hard to maintain the 'brand' across all of the campuses."

Weber is a humble leader who jokingly admits that much of the time he doesn't know up from down. He and the team have tried many strategies over the years. Operating in two states (South Dakota and Minnesota), practices that may look the same are often received differently. Each campus has the same heartbeat, but there are nuances in how ministry is carried out in each location.

The original campus in Sioux Falls has a different personality than the campus in Tea, South Dakota. Everything Weber's team has learned about doing ministry in South Dakota had to be re-imagined as they moved into Minnesota.

Adam says:

> *I've never seen the importance of contextualization more than I have since we began working in other communities. The game has changed dramatically—even in the questions we have to work to answer. There was a time where you could assume a basic knowledge of the church, and now our culture is so far removed from church that we have to approach things very differently. When I was in Kentucky, you could ask, 'Who is going to Hell,' and you might get an answer like, 'People who haven't repented.' Now the answer is more like, 'Gosh, maybe a murderer? I don't know.'*

We don't live in a world where kids graduated from confirmation class when they were in grade school, left the church, and then came back. They may never have even tried God.

This has meant that we have to try and tell people the story in a new way so they can hear it possibly for the first time, or in a brand-new way. Context is everything.

A big ah-ha moment for me is that legalism doesn't even exist for these people like it did in the past. There is such a tiny minority of people who knew what the legalistic rules are; they have no connection at all to that culture.

Adam continues to explain that, whereas everything was more uniform when Embrace began, they've now shifted strategies to allow more contextualization at their various campuses. The worship order is different. Events and service projects are different. Campus pastors are preaching live more often, and their people love it.

Adam also admits that he was once pretty intentional about being a singular voice in communication to the church. There was no live preaching outside of the main campus, where his sermons were recorded and shared with the other locations. He said:

We had a week where we didn't do video at the campuses, and the campus pastors preached. People loved it so much. It really changed my thinking. I'm now a huge proponent of using the local campus pastors to preach when it fits where we're headed with our series. I could see the gift of preaching in others, but we weren't developing it. That's been a very positive change.

While Embrace still uses video preaching to great effect, they look for opportunities to use live preaching as well.

Embrace employs consistent branding and design aesthetic across its campuses, but they've developed a local dive feel in their individual communities. Adam often reminds planters and potential planters to, "be the church God has called you to be for the people you have."

Reflection Questions:

Are there tweaks that could make your franchise feel more like a local dive? What are they?

If "context is everything," what are you doing to learn more about and embrace that context?

Another church that has really come to know the power of fresh ingredients is Melissa UMC, just outside of McKinney, Texas. This faith community began in 2012 at a school in a rural area in a relatively small community. Pastor Stacey Piyakhun tells us that early on, they would sometimes have to alert the farmer that one of the cows had knocked down the fence and needed to be wrangled away from the entrance to the school where they were meeting.

Melissa UMC began as a pretty typical mother/daughter plant model under the planting Pastor Alan Hitt. Alan has a deep passion for reaching unchurched people, and with an intentional effort to reach that crowd, the church experienced some positive early growth. However, after about 18 months, the church began to plateau as it struggled to find the right audience for the community it was situated in.

It was at that time that Pastor Stacey Piyakhun was brought

on board to bring new leadership and vision. Just before her arrival, the church experienced a decline following Easter.

Stacey says:

> *When I arrived, the attendance was around 40 people. There had been some significant decline after the initial launch, and that accelerated after Easter. People were feeling it. I was appointed mid-year, and my initial strategy was to encourage the people to dream big.*
>
> *When I began on January 1st, I asked a question that would frame the goal for our first several months together: 'What is the one thing you'd like to do before Easter of this year?' They responded by saying that they'd like to double their attendance in worship. We began efforts to make that happen by inviting friends, family and neighbors.*
>
> *With a lot of intentional work, we surpassed our goal just one week after Easter. This was a really great shot in the arm for our people.*

Under Stacey's leadership the church continued to grow. Offering a uniquely different experience than what is offered at First UMC McKinney (high church traditional and a contemporary style worship), Melissa UMC offers a worship experience that is a blend of some traditional, and some non-traditional elements.

Stacey says,

> *We have created a worship experience that the people in our context love. It's a mix of liturgical elements, but also creativity too. We like to think of it as the best of our tradition but with elements that connect to today. In a place like Melissa, it's a really great fit. Most people*

recognize that not everything in the service is going to be something they love, but they get that church is not just about our likes and preferences.

And love it they do. In 2015, a second service was added as numbers increased. The following year, the people of Melissa UMC began to dream about building their own facility. Twelve acres of land was donated and both locations began raising funds to build their new building.

It's been an exciting thing to witness the growth, but no one tells you about the perils of the middle of the journey. You're established, but not yet there. It's taken us five years to go from the dream, to architectural plans, to breaking ground and finally completion of the building. People start to lose sight of the destination. They feel like they're just hanging around waiting. They want to go back to the excitement of what it felt like when we were new. But this year, we break ground and, 6 years after the creation of our master plan, we should be moving in to our new 7600 square foot facility.

Building a new building wasn't the only consideration. Over time, the relationship with First UMC McKinney had to be rebuilt as well. Lots of work went into moving from an "us and them mentality", to an "we're all in this together" one. They did a lot of exploration to consider the nature of the relationship they were in. The church has effectively shifted from a mother/daughter relationship to more of a multi-site model.

The partnership between the two churches has benefited both locations. They're living very much into the interdependent zone on the Franchise to Local Dive Continuum.

Melissa UMC benefits from both resources and the legacy provided by First UMC McKinney. With them, we don't feel like we're on our own. There is a great peace in knowing that. We shake things up for them since we haven't "grown up" in the system. For us, they provide checks and balances on things we might miss.

The relationship has helped McKinney to not turn inward. This is a temptation for any church with a long history. They have embraced us in ways that are somewhat intangible, but our people feel welcomed there.

Since we come from a very non-traditional setting that isn't a church building, our people don't sometimes know the expected behavior that might come with a traditional. I can remember at a combined Ash Wednesday service that was held at McKinney, one of our people was excited by a moment in worship yelled out 'woohoo'. In our context this is not out of character, but in a more high-church style of space and worship, folks couldn't help but snicker a bit.

The people of McKinney are thrilled when we're together, and while our churches may have different personalities, there is a palpable sense of connection felt between our congregations.

Both congregations are thriving as one, and feel no real drive for Melissa UMC to charter to become its own independent congregation. Stacey says that they all agree that both congregations want to remain connected until that connection hinders one of the two campuses.

Having grown to nearly 200 in attendance at Melissa UMC, it is obvious that the recipe these two congregations have formed is one that we expect to keep people coming for the long haul.

Reflection Questions:

What are you doing to keep people excited and engaged in the in between time from vision/dream to completion?

How can you encourage the people who are part of your existing thing to extend love and hospitality to those doing the new thing?

If you have started something new, is one thing hindering the other? Could it be time to release that thing to become independent?

Not every church is creating a local dive by planting a brand-new campus. For many congregations, creating a local dive is more about reexamining worship services or starting new worship experiences. Worship is one of the most important ingredients in creating a local dive for a new context and new people. It is one of the most foundational elements in any recipe that seeks to engage a new community of Jesus followers.

Unfortunately, without realizing it, churches that are trying to do a new thing are often cooking with an old recipe. Their approach may be new to them, but it isn't fresh.

Often churches start with a desire to provide an alternative to "traditional worship." While a new offering may be called "contemporary" or "modern," it shares too many ingredients with the traditional experience to set it apart. You may have experienced this.

One walks into the same sanctuary, sees the same people, hears from the same pastor and lectors, looks at the same bulletin at a nearly identical liturgy, and does everything in the same order as before. But, instead of singing a hymn from the hymnal, words to the music are projected on screens. And instead of a choir or music director leading worship accompanied by an organ, worship is led by a guitarist, flautist, and perhaps a vocalist or two. This new worship consists of scaled-down (or scaled-up) songs from the past few decades instead of from the past few centuries. While new and different musical talents are often appreciated, a "new" service like this will not motivate most people beyond choosing a service based on the most convenient time for them.

During a recent consultation, Jason was working with a team launching a new contemporary worship service. When Jason asked what was going to make it contemporary, the pastor replied, "Well, it'll be a light version of our traditional service with screens and guitar and drums."

Jason responded, "Okay, but what's going to make it contemporary?" And the pastor innocently repeated the same thing he'd said before. After further conversation and another worship design session, Jason worked with the team to create something unique and different in the service. A local dive worship experience is doomed to fail if most of the ingredients are pulled from what already exists.

Reflection Questions:

What is the signature dish you plan to offer?

How will it be served up?

What will make this experience different from what currently exists?

We've seen numerous contemporary worship services crash and burn because they were not distinct and different enough from what was already offered. In his secret worshiper consultation work, Jason is often asked to evaluate worship at churches doing more than one style of worship. He often compares the liturgies of these worship expressions. Most of the churches that aren't growing are doing the same liturgy with hymns in one service and non-hymns in another.

Many formal elements of a traditional worship fit well into the traditional rubric, but fail to connect in a new paradigm. For example, "passing of the peace," greeting one another, and singing songs like the doxology fit well in a traditional service, but don't always fit in a non-traditional setting.

To add that secret sauce to keep worship fresh and engaging, ask yourself the question, "What about the experience is 'contemporary'?"

Here are a few examples that can set your new service apart:

1. **Act of service** – Consider incorporating a missional act of service as part of the worship time. We've done this by stuffing backpacks, building hygiene kits, and packing sack lunches for the homeless during songs of worship.

2. **Tactile experience** – Hand out an object and ask people to interact with it during prayer. We've handed out Play-Doh and asked people to sculpt a prayer as a symbol of how

they feel God is shaping them. We've given out baggage tags and asked people to write the burdens they needed to give to God.

We've handed out broken pieces of pottery, asked people to write prayers on them, and then had them fashioned into a mosaic art piece.

3. **Environmental projection** – Shooting a projector or projectors at the wall to immerse people in the setting of a story (biblical or otherwise) and to enhance the telling of that story.

4. **Interactive worship** – Encouraging people to live-tweet in worship where a hashtag has been established ahead of time can make for an engaging experience (and yes, they can be vetted before they go on the screen). Applications like menti.com allow you to offer real time polls. There are even apps that allow worship participants to create synchronized light shows with their phones.

5. **Break the template** – Create an entirely unique worship order. What if you started with the sermon and let every-

thing else be a response to it? Or if you divided the sermon with an intermission of singing? Start with a monologue, or a video clip, or a creative moment. Worship that is predictable is boring. Don't feel compelled to do the same thing in the same order every week.

There are many great new models for doing fresh, out-of-the-box worship. All can be tweaked to your church's liking. Consider the following movements, in their own words, for inspiration:

Fresh Expressions

A Fresh Expression is a form of church for our changing culture, established primarily for the benefit of those who are not yet part of any church.

Fresh Expressions is an international movement of missionary disciples cultivating new kinds of church alongside existing congregations to more effectively engage our growing post-Christian society.

Beginning in 2004 as an initiative of the Church of England and the British Methodist Church, the movement has resulted in the birth of thousands of new communities in the UK alone and brought renewal to scores of established churches. The movement has spread to Australia, Canada, New Zealand, South Africa, and Germany. In 2010, the movement began taking shape in the US through the vision and generosity of the Baptist General Association of Virginia and a growing number of partners committed to a new era of missional ecumenism, a unity around the mission of God the Father through the resurrected Son in the power of the Holy Spirit.

You can learn more at freshexpressionsus.org.[86]

Dinner Church Collective

Dinner Church Collective grew out of a problem that Verlon and Melodee Fosner were facing in Seattle. Their robust, storied 90-year-old church was dying a slow and quiet death.

With this gift of desperation, they began to experiment with new forms of Church. After a few missteps, they stumbled into a simple practice.

It was a practice that piqued the interest of non-Christians and Christians alike.

It was simple and affordable.

It was a practice Jesus used with his disciples.

It was a practice that the Church Fathers developed to reach and disciple believers across the ancient world.

A meal, music, and message.

In the next few years, their church reorganized around these simple principles. They now gather in 10 locations in Seattle, around a warm meal and the stories of Jesus.

Dinner Churches have grown well beyond those ten locations in Seattle and are popping up all over the U.S. To learn more visit dinnerchurch.com.[87]

Messy Church

Messy Church USA has been formed to provide an

[86] Fresh Expressions. https://freshexpressionsus.org/about/. Accessed December 18, 2019.

[87] Dinner Church Collective. https://dinnerchurch.com/about/. Accessed December 18, 2019.

organizational structure to support the health, growth, and sustainability of local Messy Churches in the USA. In addition, Messy Church USA will assist individual Messy Churches to become an integrated part of the larger national and global network of Messy Churches.

Messy Church USA is affiliated with the international Messy Church movement, whose home is with the Bible Reading Fellowship (BRF), a Christian charity based in Oxfordshire, UK.

Messy Church started in an Anglican church near Portsmouth, UK, in 2004 and has grown into an international movement operating across a wide range of Christian denominations and traditions. It became part of The Bible Reading Fellowship (BRF) in 2006 with the publication of the first Messy Church book by founder Lucy Moore.

As an affiliate of the international Messy Church movement, a guiding principle for Messy Church USA is that a local Messy Church is not a stepping stone into an existing congregation, nor is it a church plant, but it is a congregation in its own right. Messy Church is ecumenical and seeks to work with all Christian churches.

Messy Church Values

Christ-centered: Messy Church is a church, not a craft club, that helps people to encounter and enter into a transforming relationship with Jesus. Messy Church believes with the historic churches, in one God, who is Creator, Redeemer, and Sustainer (or in traditional language, Father, Son, and Holy Spirit).

All-age: Messy Church is for adults and children to enjoy together. Every element should be relevant and accessible to all ages.

Creativity: Messy Church uses hands-on activities to explore Bible stories, to reflect a God of creativity, and to give people a chance to play together.

Celebration: Messy Church reflects a God of joy who wants *all* of God's people to have life in all its fullness.

Hospitality*: Messy Church reflects a God of unconditional love and is a church for people outside of a traditional church, providing an oasis of welcome and a safe place in which to thrive. Messy Church is about hospitality, expressed most evidently by eating together - whether it's a plate of sandwiches to share, a full course meal, or pizza.

Messy church is an exciting and unique kind of faith community. To learn more visit messychurchusa.org

Alpha

Alpha is a series of sessions exploring the Christian faith, typically run over eleven weeks. Each talk looks at a different question around faith and is designed to create conversation. Alpha is run all around the globe, and everyone is welcome.

What to expect? Alpha runs in cafés, churches, universities, homes —you name it. No two Alphas look the same, but they generally have three key things in common: food, a talk, and good conversation.

First there's food: Whether it's a group of friends gathered around a kitchen table, or a quick catch-up over coffee and cake, food has a way of bringing people together. It's no

*Each Messy Church must adhere to the health and safety and safeguarding laws and guidelines applicable within its jurisdiction and operation and have established health, safety, and safeguarding policies in place that it can provide upon request. Messy Church USA and BRF cannot be held responsible for any matters related to health, safety, or safeguarding in respect of any Messy Church.

different at Alpha. We start with food, because it's a great way to encourage community and get to know each other.

Then a talk: The talks are designed to engage and inspire conversation. Generally thirty minutes long, they can be given as a live talk or played as a video. They explore the big issues around faith and unpack the basics of Christianity, addressing questions such as Who is Jesus? and How can we have faith?

Followed by a discussion: Probably the most important part of any Alpha: the chance to share thoughts and ideas on the topic and simply discuss it in a small group. There's no obligation to say anything. And there's nothing you can't say. It's an opportunity to hear from others and contribute your own perspective in an honest, friendly, and open environment.

We've both participated in Alpha, and absolutely loved what they have to offer. This local dive is especially geared toward those who are considered "nones" and "dones." In other words, those who have not yet begun a life of faith or those who have walked away from it.

Check out alpha at *alphausa.org.*

Hymns and Hops

Hymns & Hops hosted its first event in December 2016. The initial gathering had eighty people. In less than one year, it has grown to attract over 1,000 people. In November 2017, we officially became a part of and accountable to the registered non-profit, All Good Things, Inc. Hymns & Hops creates the space for families and people to celebrate the Gospel through community, song, and drink.

This local dive combines the love of God, the Gospel, and music with the love of beer and the responsible enjoyment of it. In other words, they discourage drunkenness.

Learn more here *hymnsandhops.com.*

Reflection Questions:

What could you do to reimagine worship and create something new?

What's the secret sauce that makes your new thing unique?

What are you doing to differentiate what you're doing from what you've done before?

CHAPTER 5

INCARNATIONAL MINISTRY

We are people of flavor. Jesus calls us the salt of the earth. We are called to cook something great in our communities. Finding our local flavor means knowing the people in our community. It means doing demographic research, and, even more importantly, having feet on the street, meeting the people where they are. Discovering local flavor requires cultural exegesis and the practice of getting to know our neighbors and communities, the strengths, the felt needs, and the opportunities to make a delicious recipe.

In order to do this, you have to be present among the people. Ezra was not hiding in an office, strategizing in a meeting, or even worshiping in a church service. Ezra was among the people. He was accessible for the people to call upon him to read the law. We can assume that there was some sort of relationship in place. He knew the people, his context, and understood the local flavor of his day. Ezra was intentional about placing himself in a unique position to discover the local flavor where God used him to bring revival.

Creating a recipe, the people were moved by his availability and willingness to do something that many couldn't do in his society: read the scriptures. In a day when literacy was a privilege not everyone had, Ezra was able to use his skills – as mundane as they may have seemed – to help the people understand what God desired for them. That day when he woke up to go about his work, it may have seemed like every other ordinary day of his life. He didn't know it was going to be a day that changed everything for the people.

Ezra didn't preach a sermon, give an altar call, or manipulate the crowd in any way. He just gave them what they asked for: the Word of God. Though culture has changed through the centuries, the heartfelt needs of people have not. Though the methodology of sharing the Gospel has iterated over time, the message still remains the same. People remain hungry, and our privilege is to give the people what they desire, served up with real ingredients and local flavor.

In the popular show *Diners, Drive-Ins and Dives*, the host, Guy Fieri, travels across the country to discover where the locals are dining. Fieri doesn't just stop at a restaurant for a quick meal. He talks to the local customers and the kitchen staff about the food and how it is prepared. What Fieri teaches us is that discovering the local flavor in a community requires conversation on a level that many church leaders don't take the time to do.[88]

An episode called "Local Flavor" is described like this:

> *Guy Fieri hits the road to find some of the best local favorites in the country: Off-the-hook chili from a secret family recipe at an 85-year-old Seattle joint; Crab cioppino and artichoke soup at a more than 100-year-old California bar-turned-restaurant, with a produce garden of its own; and an Oklahoma joint on Rt. 66 that serves some of the most bizarre local favorites you've ever seen.*[89]

You might notice that Fieri's destinations aren't exactly new establishments. Outside the region, they may not be known by name, but they are each famous in their local areas. Being a popular dining establishment doesn't require a restaurant being new and trendy with the latest technology and a multi-million-dollar marketing budget. These are real places, many in their original buildings, working with recipes that date back decades.

A church planter or pastor must have an affinity for their ministry context. In order to love their mission field, they must understand it. Demographic studies help, but one of

[88] *Diners, Drive-Ins and Dives*. The Food Network, 2018.

[89] Reinhardt, Christianna, et al. "Local Flavor." *Diners, Drive-Ins and Dives*, performance by Guy Fieri, season 2, episode 4, The Food Network, 22 Oct. 2007.

the best ways to get contextual is having "feet on the street." Talking to real people who live in the area and conducting informal interviews inform a planter of the strengths, needs, and opportunities in a given context. Worship styles and outreach strategies don't always translate well to every setting. What works in a suburban area may not succeed in an urban area and vice versa.

What this all boils down to is what we call "cultural exegesis." Applied to culture, *exegesis* means discovering why people in a particular culture do what they do by observing them and viewing their cultural influences from *their* perspective rather than interpreting behavior through our own cultural lenses. The opposite of exegesis is *eisegesis* (literally "to draw in"), where the observer brings meaning to the object being observed from the outside, usually formed by his or her own presuppositions.

When reading and interpreting biblical text, we can either find meaning in the text, or we can project our own meaning onto it. Both exegesis and eisegesis have valuable roles in church planting, but it is crucial to the success of a new church that its leaders develop an intentional focus on cultural exegesis. So how do we do cultural exegesis?

EMBRACE CHURCH, LEXINGTON, KY

When Roz planted his first church, Embrace Church in Lexington, Kentucky, he had no real office space. It turned out to be a blessing in disguise because it motivated him to be out in the community every day. He would meet people in local coffee shops, restaurants, and taverns.

He became a regular at several places of business, which allowed him to foster relationships with folks who wouldn't have set foot in an established church. At first, he would go in undercover because as soon as he would tell people he was a pastor, they would quit being themselves around him. His title became "Faith Community Developer" because he was trying to plant a Christian community. He met a lot of people who eventually became part of, or at least visited, Embrace Church. (The lack of office space paid off again when he ended up meeting his wife Callie at a Starbucks, of all places!)

We're not suggesting that you should give up your office if you have one, but be mindful of the temptation to be holed up with busy work at the exclusion of spending time with the very people and communities we are trying to serve. An office can be the worst enemy of a church planter - the comfort of a desk and chair, surrounded by books, protected by a closed office door. Just reading this, you're probably imagining the peace and quiet. The temptation to focus inward can be especially strong to a planter after a major letdown or rejection. You can allow the letdown to kick your butt for a day or so, but permanent retreat will not help. Make your office a public place—a coffee shop, restaurant, or anywhere you can have human interaction—for a couple of days a week, and find out what God wants to show you about your community.

A great way to start is by frequenting local establishments on a routine basis. The local movement is cause to celebrate. We're all looking around our neighborhoods for meaningful ways to connect with one another. Businesses, too, are looking for ways to give back to their local communities.

As churches, let's partner and participate in the good work our local businesses are doing. An easy way to discover the local flavor is by consistently patronizing and establishing relationships with local businesses, whether it's pizza restaurants or coffee shops on the block. It's good for the local community and it builds goodwill for the church within the community. You might begin to think of it as a potential form of disciple-making, even if all you're doing is choosing to support a local business every time you meet with someone outside the church or order in for an event.

Additionally, getting to know your business neighbors will put you in touch with the pulse of the community. You may find out about local needs. Businesses hoping to give back to their communities may come to you first for input about how they might do that.

Another idea to encourage your church to discover the local flavor is by simply offering a business directory. Again, the most powerful outcome here is connection. By providing local businesses the chance to be represented in a business directory, you offer them access to your church attendees and potential clients. Your church attendees have the ability to patronize local businesses. This builds goodwill.

Business owners and workers may end up attending the church and even investing time, finances, or skills in the church. They will also be more likely to connect others to the church if and when the need arises. Additionally, a business directory could, at the very least, pay for its own paper and printing through the sale of larger ads by businesses interested in increasing their presence.

Directories can be put together and printed by someone at your church, or might also provide for mutually beneficial opportunities to partner with others. When a strong level of mutual understanding has been established between a church and a local business, and when the two share common values, a partnership can multiply God's work in our communities.

Reflection Questions:

How much time are you spending in your office versus out in the field?

How have you gotten to know the local businesses in your area?

When Roz moved from Kentucky to Dayton, Ohio, he became a campus pastor of The Point Church in Trotwood, Ohio (a campus of Ginghamsburg Church). He had to hit the ground running. One of the first things he did was police ride-alongs.

If you want to know what's going on in your community, a police ride-along is an eye-opening experience. Moments after jumping in the cruiser, it occurred to Roz that it wouldn't be completely impossible to have one of his parishioners pulled over while he was in the car. That would have been awkward! Luckily, in all of his ride-alongs, that never happened.

Roz went into this ride with much intentionality. As he and the police officer were riding around the city, he casually asked the three questions:

1. **What are the greatest strengths of this community?**
2. **What are the greatest needs?**
3. **What are the opportunities?**

The officer's response to the first question was, "togetherness." Roz learned that Trotwood had a sense of town pride and was a tightknit community. The long-term citizens are trying to reclaim Trotwood after tough years of crime and recession.

The officer's response about the greatest needs in Trotwood was something Roz had heard before: children and teenagers needed activities. As the officer continued to share about the community, Roz could see a need for a community center type atmosphere with relevant music, games, food, and access to positive role models.

Roz immediately recognized there was plenty of space to start a community center in the shopping strip where The Point was located. He also knew that there were plenty of empty commercial spaces available throughout Trotwood.

After his ride-along, Roz asked these same three questions to longtime residents, community leaders, and the mayor. Their answers led Roz to the strategy that sports were going to be a huge opportunity for rallying together. Those conversations also illuminated opportunities to partner in or create activities for children, youth, and the entire community.

The discoveries a planter makes while doing incarnational ministry will begin to define the church's outreach/mission, vision, values, worship style, and ministry opportunities. Context is crucial and must prayerfully be considered as the planter begins to see the mission field clearly. Context will determine the collective personality of a worshiping community, what style of worship they love, and what kinds of ministry will resonate in the community. Ministry opportunities in line with the local flavor, like those listed below, can emerge through informal interviews.

Birthed in 2009, Urban Village church has really leaned into what it means to be incarnation in the way that they do ministry in this present time. They have four locations spread throughout Chicagoland - each with its own flavor - while sharing a common vision.

We talked to Emily McGinley, who is the planting/campus

pastor for Urban Village's fourth location (Hyde Park-Woodlawn) as well as the executive pastor of Urban Village as a whole. She shared with us how contextual ministry has been a key strategy in growing a healthy church.

> *I came to Urban Village from the Presbyterian church, without ever having thought much about planting. I had a heart for congregational revitalization, and at the time I was working as the executive director for a program called Common Ground that supported young adults of color who were exploring ministry. That program was coming to its end, when I happened to meet Chris Coon, one of the founding pastors of Urban Village.*

Urban Village had planted three locations and begun to think about what planting another congregation should look like in a largely segregated city. The existing campuses had all been planted in predominately white neighborhoods and after attending an anti-racism summit, the pastors and lay leaders who had attended, committed to plant the next site in a part of the city that had a greater possibility for racial diversity.

> *I lived in the Hyde Park area and Chris asked if I thought a church like Urban Village could work in this part of the city. I began to get very excited about the possibility about what Chris and Trey Hall (the other co-pastor) were exploring as it lined up with the two halves of my faith experience. Those halves being a more evangelical tradition that emphasized personal, engaged, discipleship and accountability, and a more progressive theology that emphasized critical thinking and faithful engagement of the systems and structures we live in.*
>
> *I got excited about how this could be a church that centered on meeting the spiritual needs and experiences of*

LGBTQ people of color on the south side of the city, mainly because the inverse is what is usually available to them.

I also realized that this area is a place where people are very transient and disconnected and so it's really easy to be lonely. The thought of cultivating a container where folks could connect in a deeper and more authentic way with one another, while figuring out what it means to follow in the way of Jesus, was very exciting to me.

I agreed to join the staff and build this fourth campus from the ground up with this context in mind.

In starting its fourth site, Urban Village did the hard work of building relationships within the city. The area in which it was planted was much more racially diverse than the other campuses already in existence. There was an intentionality about the cultural touchpoints they drew from when establishing this new faith community. Things had to look different at this site than the other campuses, yet still be aligned with the mission and vision of Urban Village as a whole.

With a full commitment to living into its mission to be truly inclusive, an 18-month anti-racism audit was conducted. The audit helped Urban Village Church's leadership to see the ways that were –and were not– fully living into their stated commitment to inclusivity. It also gave them concrete ideas on how to make sure systems could be put in place to do even better.

A lot of contextualization happens in worship even though series are shared across all campuses. For instance, the music at each location offers a distinct expression. In our location, given our context and who is worshiping with us, contemporary gospel music is emphasized. At other campuses you may hear more of a Hillsong vibe, or contemporary Christian music.

Contextualization also happens in the sermon. Each pastor takes the bigger, "umbrella" ideas that are being emphasized overall, and makes relevant to the congregation they're being shared with.

The leaders at Urban Village have also been doing intentionally incarnational ministry by building meaningful relationships within their various communities.

Some of the things we've done have involved partnering with local businesses that match our vibe as a church. We've done 'Open Mic Night' at a local business that sells and promotes local art and other merchandise that appeals to our core demographic.

One member of our staff came up with the idea of Tattoo Testimonies. A lot of folks in our communities have tattoos and there are some amazing stories embedded with those images. We partnered with a tattoo shop, where people were invited to come and tell their stories. We then used a small grant we had received to subsidize folks getting a tattoo if they wanted one.

At first the owner was a bit skeptical and maybe even a little suspicious, but after he experienced the stories, he was blown away and was so glad to be a part of it.

Finally, since even before we launched, we've offered a pre-Christmas Eve service in a local coffee shop. Since many of our congregants are young adults, they often go home for Christmas to be with family. This service takes place a few days before Christmas Eve, and gives us a chance to experience Christmas with our Urban Village family. It's a win-win because the coffee shop is a great host, and we are providing customers for them during a time when fewer customers are coming in.

It's also kind of nice because the fact that it's a public service means those in the community or who have just come in for a cup sometimes join in.

The feet on the street ethos of Urban Village, has been part of its winning recipe. They've built a church around the specific needs of their community. This thriving church is thinking toward the future and creating even more faith communities in other locations.

As Urban Village demonstrates, ministry opportunities must fall in line with the local flavor. Getting out into the community and interviewing folks will provide you with a plethora of opportunity. Here is a list of just some of the things you might attempt to do to put your cultural exegesis into practice:

After-school programs: By allowing space for after-school programs to meet and encouraging your laity to get involved with the work, the church can both bring more kids and their parents through their doors than they otherwise might. This creates opportunities to serve kids in the area who need an extra meal, tutoring, encouragement, healthy relationships, and a safe space for fun.

Job and life skills mentorship programs: As a church, we're not only concerned with helping people who are living in poverty, we want to help people out of poverty! There are many programs across the country offering adults the job and life skills they need to break out of poverty. Churches can offer job and life skills programs in their space to meet along with servants to teach, mentor, counsel, and encourage participants. This win-win solution allows the church meaningful service opportunities while simultaneously allowing organizations with successful models to continue their effective work!

Music education programs: As public schools face budget cuts and let go of their arts programs, organizations all over the country have sprung up to offer students affordable or free music lessons. In order to keep their own costs low, these programs often need practice and performance space. Imagine your entire sanctuary filled with people who don't attend Sunday church services taking in a performance you're hosting. This affords you the ability to greet them with warmth and hospitality. It also provides the chance to begin building meaningful relationships.

Local radio stations: Radio stations often sponsor or conduct their own fundraising events, and are looking for space or even volunteers to assist. Secular radio stations can provide awareness of your ministries with groups of people who may not be familiar with your church. Partnering with local stations can send the message that you care and are invested in the community.

Community events: Perhaps you have a great idea for an event you'd like to offer your community, but lack the funding to make it a reality. Check your community calendar from prior years. There are very likely similar events that are already planned whose organizers would love to have what you can offer in the way of volunteers and other possibilities (pitch in a hot-dog stand, for example). These things could be offered in exchange for double-billing of the event!

Garden/Urban farming programs: Local and urban farming initiatives are popping up all across the country.

These markets are serving as much needed oases in what have become food deserts. They are alleviating the lack of access to fresh, healthy, organic food. Many have educational camps or programs designed to teach our next generations how to grow, harvest, and prepare their own foods. Hook up with one of these local groups to find out how you can get involved!

Food pantry/access programs: Your church may not have its own food pantry, but it can serve as a distribution center for existing food access programs. Every church can collect canned goods and non-perishable items.

Crisis organizations: There are numerous organizations across the country already in place which provide necessities to those in financial or medical crisis. Likewise, churches will inevitably come across people in need. Establishing a partnership with these organizations can streamline the process of getting needed aid to church members. It can also provide the organizations with office space and/or co-fund community awareness initiatives.

Recovery organizations: As Christians, we are all "in recovery." But those who are in recovery from drugs, alcohol, and other addictions need support from recovery organizations as well as from their local churches. Again, many very successful recovery organizations already exist in our towns and cities, but need safe spaces to meet. In many cases, the participants in these programs are required to attend a local church for community and accountability.

Local schools: Many of the churches Roz has pastored have formed partnerships with local schools. A great source for exploring ideas on how to partner with local schools is Adam McClane's article, "10 Ways Your Church Can Be Good News to Public Schools."[90]

Local police departments: The church can be a great place to connect police officers and the public they serve on neutral ground. Invite your local force to take part in events such as a community kickball tournament. These kinds of partnerships are badly needed in our country today where relations between law enforcement and communities can be strained. Roz found that organizing a community kickball tournament was easier than he thought it might be. The relationships that form between the church and police officers are invaluable. The mutually beneficial relationships and ongoing communication can help drive what types of outreach are needed in your community.

Reflection Questions:

What are you doing to challenge yourself and your team to live into your stated mission?

Cultural exegesis is not just for church planters but also for pastors and lay people. If you truly care about your community, it's time to get out of the office and into the mission field. As founder of Methodism John Wesley said, "The world is my parish."

When Roz was planting his first church in Lexington, Kentucky, there was an old gymnasium in a downtown area that the church planned to purchase after being in a rented movie theater for three years. The gym had showers, locker

---

[90] AdamMcLane.com. "10 Ways Your Church Can Be Good News to Public Schools." http://adammclane.com/2010/09/07/good-news-to-public-schools/. Accessed December 18, 2019.

rooms, and room for growth. They had a contract on the building, but at the zoning hearing the neighbors protested against the church because the ministry of their church was often to folks on the margins of society. The protesters didn't want any more of "those people" in their neighborhood. Prior to this, in the same town, another church had wanted to move into an old bread factory. They encountered the same resistance. That factory is now a microbrewery.

In the 1990s, public schools were great places for church plants, but in some communities, the landscape has also changed for the worse. Unless you're moving into an existing building that has already been zoned for a church, space is hard to come by.

Alan Hirsch and Michael Frost pointed out in *The Shaping of Things to Come* that, "what is needed is the abandonment of the strict lines of demarcation between the sacred and profane spaces in our world and the recognition that people today are searching for relational communities that offer belonging, empowerment, and redemption." Hirsch and Frost then lay out four characteristics of missional church models. One that has resonated with us in our post-Christian world—and which I believe can help future church planters to think outside the box—is what Hirsch and Frost call *proximity spaces*. These are "places or events where Christians and not-yet-Christians can interact meaningfully with each other."[91] This can involve developing cafes, nightclubs, art galleries, design studios, etc.

We often assume incorrectly that the only place Christians can meet with God or receive divine revelations is inside a church. Moving forward, this line of demarcation must

[91] Frost, Michael, and Alan Hirsch. "The Missional Church." *The Shaping of Things to Come: Innovation and Mission for the 21st-Century Church*, Baker Books, 2013, 33–41.

disappear. Interactions between Christians and not-yet-Christians are essential for the next movement within post-Christianity. Outside-the-box thinking is imperative when it comes to spaces where people gather together for worship and live a life of service as one.[92]

To discover local flavor means to be mobile. One of the most quoted Scriptures in the Church has been known as the Great Commission. It is found in Matthew 28:19-20:

> *Therefore go and make disciples of all nations, baptizing them in the name of the Father and of the Son and of the Holy Spirit, and teaching them to obey everything I have commanded you. And surely, I am with you always, to the very end of the age (NIV).*

As Roz reflects on the word "go" in verse 19, he has always been intrigued. We often think this means to leave our hometown, go across town, or maybe even take a mission trip to another country. All of that "going" is important. However, the more accurate translation of this phrase, "as you go," has Roz thinking differently about Jesus' command. As you go, make disciples. Is this the difference between taking on life as a mission and going on mission? What if we went about our days differently, with making disciples in mind? We can make disciples in many settings.

The most recent church Roz helped plant, Mosaic, meets in a movie theater. This is what sociologists call a "third space." The first space is commonly a person's home, where they spend most of their time. The second space is a person's place of employment. The third space is where people hang out for leisure, like a café, library, or park.

There is something about being in a third space that puts people at ease. A movie theater is a nonthreatening place.

---

[92] Ibid.

People associate the smell of popcorn and relaxing seats with a movie theater. The theater has also become a place on Sunday mornings where people have encountered God's presence and love. Even some of the employees at The Rave Cinemas have joined in on some of the worship.

Reflection Question:

What third spaces are available in your area and how might you use them to reach an audience who might never walk into a church building?

Getting to know your community and those third spaces is important because the local dive you create for that community may not even serve your favorite food. While it's important to have congruency with the community in which you choose to launch or relaunch, the nuances of the community may not line up in every way with what you have in mind for your ideal church. Your recipe must balance your tastes and sensibilities with those of the community.

Our friend Jacob Armstrong, pastor of Providence Church put it like this, "The biggest miss in creating a new church is to create one that you like." He went on to describe how, if he had his way, his church would have a cool, hip name, would play a certain style of music, people might dress a certain way, and the worship experience might look more like what he grew up with than something really out of the box. He continued saying, "That would likely be all wrong for our community."

Jacob, who is one of the most authentic and down-to-earth pastors you'll ever meet said his team avoided being slick at every turn. They named the church Providence Church after

PROVIDENCE CHURCH, MT. JULIET, TN

the community they're in – nothing overly creative, flashy, or trendy. Being smack dab in the middle of the bible belt - including "church" made great sense. He explained, "After a lot of contextual observation, we were really intentional to create a church that was a reflection of where we live and who we are."

Early in Jacob's ministry, he felt called to be a missionary. He trained for this work not knowing the value it would one day bring to his work as a church planter. Many of the same ideals and methodologies learned in his preparation for missionary work applied to doing work right here in the local context.

"We began a season of listening and learning from the people in our community," he said. "We'd walk through neighborhoods, eat at local restaurants, hang out, see what people were up to, and what they liked to do."

Planters, Jacob says, often feel like they have to connect with a ton of people, but sometimes it's about connecting with one person who is already a connector. He reminded us of Luke 10, where Jesus sends out the seventy-two. Jesus instructs us to look for places of peace. Finding those people of peace – those key relationships – can help a new movement grow very quickly. It really is taking on a missionary mindset as you meet people in the community.

Providence began meeting in schools, city parks, hotels, and so on in its early years. For eight years, they were a mobile church which really put an emphasis on relationships and people. Jacob reflected on those early days, "When you're meeting in a smelly middle school gym, you know it's all about relationships and the people gathered and not the space."

When Providence had grown to the point where it made sense to build its own facility, it was important to think again about the recipe they were creating. Jacob shared that they had to revisit some of the work they'd done ten years earlier to relearn the community and consider the ways in which it had changed.

They also went out of their way to create a space that wasn't overly fancy, but had a flavor more like those early school rooms that the community was birthed in than some kind of cutting-edge theater. He stresses that their DNA is not about building buildings, but about people.

And while it's not about the building, the new space did allow the church to grow. They nearly doubled in attendance after moving in.

Providence is thriving, and you might think that would be enough. It would be easy to rest on its laurels and maintain what has been built. Believing in the church, Jacob and his leaders shared a vision for even greater kingdom impact.

Providence Church - a church plant - was ready to plant another campus. But rather than franchise what they had built and create a near duplicate church in another location, they decided to do something that is almost unheard of in the church planting world: adopt a new campus with a different name, setting, and worship style. There are almost no overt references to Providence (the planting church) at the new venue led by pastor Jason McAnally. In fact, Jacob estimates that only 20 percent of the congregation even knows that the campus is an offshoot of Providence.

Rather than plant Providence West, the new venue is an almost fully autonomous new faith community called Home Church.

As Jacob put it, "The local dive is incarnational. We

HOME CHURCH, NASHVILLE, TN

wanted this new faith community to be what it needed to be for this community. Not just something we imposed on them from our area."

When you visit Home Church, you'll see a renovated older sanctuary where the pulpit has been removed, loft has been yanked out, floors redone, modern projection and lighting technology present, and an overall mix of classic architecture and modern-day styling. The seats are filled with passionate worshipers, who tend to skew younger. There are lots of millennials present each week.

This congregation looks different than what you'll find at the planting campus, a reality that Jacob and his leaders celebrate. The intention from the beginning was to create a local dive that is supported by a healthy church with resources that made something new possible. And both congregations are thriving because of their unique recipes.

Reflection Questions:

Do you love your new recipe so much that you may need to rethink it a bit? Is it too much about your likes/dislikes and not enough about those you're trying to reach?

In naming your new recipe, are you reaching for something trendy or are you embracing what's natural for your context?

If you're a franchisor looking to create something new, what are the potential upsides and downsides to birth something that doesn't have overt ties back to the franchise?

As Jacob and Jason and their respective churches demonstrate, discovering the local flavor of a community means thinking of ourselves as missionaries. We must take the time to learn the language, customs, culture, to ask questions, and simply listen. The American church needs to rediscover the biblical understanding of living missionally in a post-Christian culture. It doesn't take a rocket scientist to figure out that many of the churches in the United States are plateauing or declining. The rate of church closures will continue to ramp up. Young people ages 18 to 35 are virtually a missing demographic, and more are turning away from the church. The same people who have divorced themselves from the church wear crosses around their necks, sport tattoos with theological origins, and love Jesus but don't want anything to do with the church.

This bears resemblance to the difficult terrain that the twentieth-century Methodist missionary, E. Stanley Jones, had to cross as he was reaching out to the people of India.

Jones began his mission work among the lowest class of people. He did not attack the predominant religions of the area, but tried to present the Gospel of Jesus Christ without attaching Western culture to it. As the Methodist Board of Missions' "Evangelist-at-Large" to India, Jones conducted large meetings in Indian cities. He presided over round table conferences where people of all faiths could sit down as equals and share their testimonies of how their religious experiences improved their lives.

It could be argued that the effectiveness of Jones's mission in India—seeking to separate Jesus from Christianity—would not have been possible without the figure of Gandhi as a prime exemplar. Jones wrote:

> *I bow to Mahatma Gandhi, but I kneel at the feet of Christ and give him my full and final allegiance. And yet a little man who fought a system in the framework of which I stand, has taught me more of the spirit of Christ than perhaps any other man in East or West.*[93]

Martin Luther King, Jr. later said it was Jones' book, *The Christ of the Indian Road*, that introduced him to Gandhi and the centrality of nonviolence in Christian discipleship.

Jones once asked Gandhi how to naturalize Christianity into India. Gandhi replied in part:

> *First, I would suggest that all of you Christians, missionaries, and all, must begin to live more like Jesus Christ. Second, practice your religion without adulterating it or toning it down. Third, emphasize love and make it your working force, for love is central in Christianity. Fourth, study the non-Christian religions more sympathetically to find the good that is within them, in order to have a more sympathetic approach to the people.*[94]

Jones' ministry soon became influential worldwide as he stressed that the reconciliation brought through Jesus Christ was intended for the whole world. He helped to reestablish the

---

[93] Jones, E. Stanley. *Mahatma Ghandi: An Interpretation* (London: Hodder & Stoughton, 1948), 12.

[94] Jones, E. Stanley. "The Great Hindrance." The Christ of the Indian Road, Abingdon Press, 1925, 101–122.

Indian *Ashram* (forest retreat) where men and women would come together for days at a time to explore each other's faiths. Jones would later go on to establish Christian Ashrams around the world.[95]

Jones' reputation as a "reconciler" earned him a place at many political negotiations in India, Africa, and Asia. He was a close confidant of U.S. President Franklin D. Roosevelt in the time preceding World War II, and after the war, he was greeted in Japan as the Apostle of Peace. He played an important role in establishing religious freedom in the post-colonial Indian government. Jones had a strong influence in preventing the spread of communism in India. Jones died in India on January 25, 1973. A prominent Methodist Bishop called E. Stanley Jones "the greatest Christian missionary since St. Paul."[96]

Jones demonstrates what it means to discover the local flavor with missiological methods. Jones depended on the locals to understand the people of India before trying to impose his views on the people. In his relationship with Ghandi he was able to discover how the native people viewed Christ and Christianity, and was able to contextualize the Gospel in a way that preserved the integrity and intent of the message.

This didn't happen by happenstance. Jones took a methodical approach, almost like Guy Fieri's approach to local foods: asking questions, taking time to learn, and, most importantly, exercising deep listening.

A modern example of discovering the local flavor of a

---

[95] Ibid, 60.

[96] Kinnell, Matt. "E. Stanley Jones." www.asbury.edu/academics/resources/library/archives/biographies/e-stanley-jones/. Accessed December 18, 2019.

community comes from a church plant in western Ohio. The church is called Engage Newark, and is under the leadership of Dave Warner. At a time when Warner felt he was just as likely to leave his town as not, he began to feel a pull toward the downtown area in Newark. As he describes it, the city was already experiencing revitalization, block-by-block, as an EPA-mandated sewer system cleanup got underway. He began to ask, "What could we do to be downtown?"

LITTLE ARROWS PLAY CAFE, NEWARK, OH

Then he met a local businessman who planned to buy a block of buildings, including a ballroom where Engage Newark would eventually worship. The man's invitation to Warner was this. He explained to Warner that his girlfriend was a single mom with a three-year-old son. The mom was studying to become a nurse, and had nowhere to study while her son could play and be watched. So, she took him regularly to a McDonald's PlayPlace. The man asked Warner, "Can the church do better?" This question directed Warner's thoughts, planning, research, and finally his concrete steps. Research conducted during this time confirmed the community's specific felt need, calling the demographics of the area "Diapers and Debit Cards." Four years later, with God's faithfulness showing up in funding and timing, Warner and his team opened Little Arrows Café.

Warner describes Little Arrows Café as a place:

...where we can be the church on a daily basis connecting to the community - not just on Sundays. Rooted in a deeply

held belief in relational discipleship, a cultural need for rest and communal space and the empowerment of people of all ages, genders and races, Little Arrows provides for families with young children in our community in unique ways unlike any other church in our region.[97]

Warner and Engage Newark continue to make hundreds of contacts each month because of their interactions with children and parents, a large percentage of whom are not affiliated with a church. It's a draw in the community, meeting a need of young families for a positive and safe interaction. Little Arrows Café truly lives up to its vision:

To improve the lives of those in our community while providing a safe environment for children and parents alike. We are a place for children to play and for parents to connect. We are aimed toward children ages 3-8. Regular hours are intended for parents and children to enjoy the space together or separately. Setup up your laptop and pour yourself a coffee while the kids enjoy the many activities the cafe provides.[98]

Little Arrows Café gauges its community in order to be a local dive from its original conception to the way it practices little details. Warner explains that knowing there are two coffee shops within walking distance, Little Arrows cannot and doesn't wish to compete with them. The coffee at Little Arrows is single-serve and low-cost. The friendly atmosphere allows people to make themselves at home affordably. The

---

[97] Warner, Dave. "About Engage Newark." www.engagenewark.com/about/. December 18, 2019.

[98] Little Arrows Play Café. www.laplaycafe.com/prices. "Pricing," Accessed December 18, 2019.

cost of all-day childcare is $3 a child. Snacks and drinks are a buck each. An annual pass costs $100, and a monthly pass costs just $30. Additionally, while Little Arrows Café is a ministry of Engage Newark and has certainly led guests to become worshipers at the church, the café first meets tangible needs of the community, allowing discipleship to happen gradually and organically.

Reflection Question:

In addition to the more in the box offerings a new faith community might offer, how might your new local dive create a much-needed opportunity or resource for your neighborhood?

CHAPTER 6

FOSTERING COLLABORATION

Everything that leads to putting a meal on the table is communal, from growing or producing the food, to sitting down and breaking bread. But what happens when there are too many cooks in the kitchen? A franchised approach offers the convenience of premade, individually weighed, and packaged foods. It lets teamwork off the hook with pre-designated roles, cook-times, and expectations, set by someone far away in a centralized test kitchen.

On the other hand, when a local dive prepares a meal, teamwork is essential. Sure, there are still routines established and maintained through the years. But every week, the chef and the staff will decide, based on the ingredients available to them, what to put on their menu and how to prepare it. In order to successfully move from a franchise to a local dive mentality in worship and ministry, church leaders must recognize that it is the function of each individual, not the title or position, that matters most. It is crucial to focus on the best recipe and how best to accomplish it together.

In the case of Ezra's prophetic preaching, his marathon sermon was accompanied by deep teaching. Nehemiah 8:8-9a says, "They read from the Book of the Law of God and clearly explained the meaning of what was being read, helping the people understand each passage. Then Nehemiah the governor, Ezra the priest and scribe, and the Levites who were interpreting for the people..." (NLT). Small group leaders were interacting with people in the crowd, explaining Scripture and answering their questions. In some translations we see the words, "making it clear" or "translating it." The Hebrew here means to make something distinct, to separate it from something else so as to make it flow together in a meaningful fashion.[99] Ezra would not have been able to effectively

---

[99] Fensham, Frank Charles. "Further Reforms of Ezra." *The Books of Ezra and Nehemiah,* Eerdmans, 2007, 96.

reach the community without the help of his team. They were able to contextualize and interpret the Scriptures for the people in the large crowd.[100] According to Old Testament Scholar H. H. Schaefer, "We must recognize that the Jews who spoke Aramaic needed someone to translate the Hebrew of the law for them in their own vernacular."[101] The results were outstanding, as seen in verse 9, "Then Nehemiah the governor, Ezra the priest and scribe, and the Levites who were interpreting for the people said to them, 'Don't mourn or weep on such a day as this! For today is a sacred day before the Lord your God.' For the people had all been weeping as they listened to the words of the Law" (NLT).

Ezra teaches us that disciples aren't made in a franchise model where one meal fits all. Many pastors have become so focused on denominational and ecclesiastical pressures to mass-produce and increase numbers that they have resorted to fast food instead of unique recipes with local flavor.

Local flavor means using real ingredients. This is not a solo mission. The work of the local dive has to be a team effort. During the height of the church growth era and the boom of the megachurch, one dynamic leader would receive the vision "on the mountaintop" and bring it down to the people. In order to return the work of ministry to the people, leadership must happen in teams.

In a recent conversation, Rev. Dr. Yvette Massey admitted that she learned this lesson much later in her ministry than she would have preferred to. She shares:

> *"As a visionary leader, it's easy to come in with the desire to move things quickly in a new direction. When a church*

---

[100] Luther, James, May et al. "Scene One: Joyous Renewal." *Interpretation: A Bible Commentary for Teaching and Preaching*, John Knox Press, 1982, 123.

[101] Fensham, 217.

is struggling, a pastor can mistakenly move without first building trust. It's imperative that relationships are built and that the movement forward is done in such a way that others are involved. You have to help the church see that they need to change. It can't just be the pastor driving the change, but the people have to be involved too.

In the African American community, there is an intricate network of relationships hierarchy that one must navigate in order to get the necessary buy-in to enact change. Within that network are the formal leaders (those elected by the church's administrative structure) and the informal leaders (those who the congregation consistently look to for leadership and influence the decision making of the church that must be sold on the vision for it to move forward. Forming partnerships with these two groups makes the work a bottom up, rather than a top down movement."

Yvette has served a number of African American churches and has gained a reputation for being a bit of a change agent. In fact, amongst some of her friends and family, she's earned the nickname "The Fixer". She has learned the value of strategically involving leaders and other team members in order to make hard things happen. She has also learned that when you skip that, people resist.

"Years ago, at one of the congregations I was pastoring, I was trying to help the choir reach the next level and added an accompanist and a director to help them improve. One outspoken choir member expressed her skepticism with this decision by asking why we need someone out in front waiving their hands around. She felt it was unnecessary, but I knew it would help them become even more unified and in sync.

After some of the grumbles and critiques were made known to me, I decided to take another approach. It wasn't until I got to one of the powerhouse leaders of the church and explained what I was trying to do and why, that everything turned around. This key leader helped me achieve buy-in amongst the rest of the choir and everything turned around. And they did very much improve, just as I'd hoped.

I just had to take a different approach that was less pastor driven and more people driven. When you get the right people on board, they help parlay the church in the right direction."

Yvette now serves as an associate director of congregational excellence at the North Georgia Conference of the United Methodist. It's her job to help churches improve what they're doing in ministry in numerous ways. It's a great ministry for a fixer.

Succession planning for solo leaders ready to retire or called to another church or ministry has become difficult. Instead of being seen as "too many cooks in the kitchen," we should recognize that effective teams provide continuity to a faith community. Teams can provide checks and balances, filter ideas, and bring out the very best.

Ideas come and go. In Roz's experience, great ideas rarely come when you sit down to meet a deadline. They come when you least expect them. Some of Roz's ideas come to him when he's mowing the lawn or taking a shower. This may sound weird, but that's when he has a chance to let his mind wander outside the lines. Roz often says that his best ideas, however, aren't his own. They are born in a team environment where collaboration is welcomed and fostered. It doesn't matter who receives the credit as long as all glory goes to God.

This has been Jason's experience as well. Jason has been working in collaborative processes for more than twenty years with dozens of teams and has found that the impact on creativity of multiple players is exponential.

This is true in any creative environment, from the church to the secular world. In addition to Jason's work in the church, he does secular freelance work that sometimes involves working with Hollywood writers and producers.

In 2016, Jason was invited to speak at a yearly event called UMC Lead. This Ted Talk style event was taking place in Los Angeles the year Jason was invited to present. He thought, *Why not include a panel of film and television writers to inspire pastors to tell better stories through their sermons?*

HOLLYWOOD WRITERS' PANEL, LOS ANGELES, CA

Jason put out a call to all of his writer and producer friends, and five agreed to be on the panel: Rob Kutner (writer for *The Daily Show* and *The Conan O'Brien Show*), Jon E. Steinberg (creator/writer/producer of *Jericho, Human Target,* and *Black Sails*), Stephen Scaia (writer/producer for *Jericho, Human Target, Limitless,* and co-creator of *Blood & Treasure*), Eric Champnella (writer for *Mr. 3000* and *Thunderstruck* and director of *Alex and Me*), and Jeffrey Berman (writer for *J.K. Rowlings Story* and creator of *The Write Environment*).

The panel of writers bantered about the process of collaborating on film and tv scripts, and two ideas kept resurfacing. First, the writers found they agreed on the notion that the story you tell has to move you first. Second, all that matters is that the best idea wins.

The panelists explained that in every scripted television show, there is a group of writers who "break the season." This means they brainstorm what will happen with the characters and narratives throughout the episodes included in that season. Those episodes are then assigned to the writers to create individual scripts. (A side note: this is an excellent approach for developing sermon series for churches with multiple preachers.)

At the top of the hierarchy in a writer's room is the executive producer or showrunner. He/she is the boss, and makes the final calls. At the bottom of that hierarchy is the writers' assistant. This person makes sure there are dry erase markers, sharpened pencils, the correct Starbucks coffee orders, and so on. They do occasionally, however, get to participate in the conversation.

More than once during the panel discussion, panelists insisted that it doesn't matter whose idea it is—whether it's the writers' assistant's idea or the showrunner's idea—the best idea wins. This idea was supported in an interview with Steven Spielberg who once said, "I don't care if the idea comes from the caterer. If it's a good idea, it's going in the movie."

How can a church foster a creative environment where the best ideas win? In 2009, Jason Moore and Len Wilson devoted an entire book to this topic entitled *Taking Flight With Creativity: Worship Design Teams That Work*. Check it out for a deep dive into collaborative design teams.

When a team is gelling and firing on all cylinders, you will typically see some of the following elements.

Safety

Teams should strive to create an environment that welcomes everybody's voice and where individuals don't fear being attacked. Most of us can recall a time we have experienced the opposite of safety in a collaborative creative process. Perhaps we were ridiculed or attacked for an idea we were throwing out. When intentional steps aren't taken, people are made to feel unsafe to contribute their ideas. They will remain silent if they don't feel safe to share. When that happens, we can eliminate an important voice in the creative conversation or decision. It doesn't matter what role individuals play, or what setting this takes place in. Once safety is gone, it is hard for people to reengage in a process that leaves them vulnerable to being hurt.

Establishing a safe environment makes room for good and bad ideas, and believe it or not, we need bad ideas. They lead to good ideas. When people aren't feeling safe, they won't risk potentially bad ideas.

In his article "McDonald's Theory," author Jon Bell describes the importance of bad ideas. This is his common practice:

> *I use a trick with co-workers when we're trying to decide where to eat for lunch and no one has any ideas. I recommend McDonald's.*
>
> *An interesting thing happens. Everyone unanimously agrees that we can't possibly go to McDonald's, and better lunch suggestions emerge. Magic!*
>
> *It's as if we've broken the ice with the worst possible idea, and now that the discussion has started, people suddenly get very creative. I call it the McDonald's Theory: people are inspired to come up with good ideas to ward off bad ones.*

He goes on to say:

The next time a project is being discussed in its early stages, grab a marker, go to the board, and throw something up there. The idea will probably be stupid, but that's good! McDonald's Theory teaches us that it will trigger the group into action.[102]

In order for people to feel safe, they need to know each other. Outings from the workplace can help foster community. Intentional trainings like an obstacle course, an escape room, or just having fun in someone's backyard can help break the ice. Instead of a regular old staff meeting, Roz's team tries to change up their format and location so they don't get caught in a rut, which ultimately aids the creative process. Another suggestion is to take time at each gathering to allow one or two teammates to share their stories, upbringing, and faith journeys and to lead in prayer and devotions.

Additionally, assessments like StrengthsFinder 2.0, Enneagram typology, and others can go a long way toward building team cohesion. Prior to the launch of Mosaic Church, Roz's staff took the StrengthsFinder 2.0 assessment. The team has benefited in multiple ways. First, it helped team members see their own value in unexpected ways. There are powerful narratives in society about personality traits that are "good" and personality traits that are "bad." But a closer look can show that someone who is shy or even standoffish may actually have super-strong listening skills or an ability to include others like themselves. Someone's "flakiness" might be better understood as a strength to sell an idea or strategy and bring others onboard, even if they aren't the best person to complete all the follow-through steps. Understanding our inherent strengths, tendencies, and motivations can help us

---

[102] Bell, John. Medium.com. "McDonald's Theory." https://medium.com/@jonbell/mcdonalds-theory-9216e1c9da7d. April 29, 2013.

see more clearly the work God has intended us to do.

Second, doing this assessment together helped Roz's team see how each of their strengths fit together in the group. This has led to more effective collaboration and decreased friction caused by personality differences. A better understanding of self leads simultaneously to a greater appreciation for the vast array of strengths, as well as to a greater tolerance for the way people do things differently than we do.

Third, the assessments revealed to Roz's team some potential blind spots. For example, a team may include several members who bring enthusiasm and fearlessness to new endeavors, but what about the person who naturally sees risk and potential pitfalls, or the person who has the discipline for the less glamorous but crucial steps, or the person who can put scaffolding beneath a shared dream with effective strategy? Without these people, a team is likely to encounter obstacles that could have been avoided, will never follow through, or will fail to meet their potential.

Safety is something we find in friendships where trust exists. In addition to collaborating on this book, Roz and Jason are frequent ministry collaborators and find some of their best work comes from brainstorming together. Jason has coached and led teams of all shapes and sizes. Reflecting on what he's learned in the last several years (when Roz made the move to Dayton) one of the things he had to learn was how to improve his weekend teachings. In small to midsize churches, pastors do a bit of everything, and Roz was no exception. When he had more opportunities to preach, he knew that he had to take his preaching to the next level as his 30-minute sermon might be the only experience people would have with him. Jason became Roz's coach. Jason's coaching was honest because he wanted Roz to do his best. There was a level of safety in this relationship because Roz knew and trusted that each of Jason's critiques were given in a spirit of friendship and truly wanting to see Roz do his best. Roz has also been a sounding board for Jason and speaks freely with him based on the safe space the two have established.

Out of safety, the two began to collaborate on a number of ideas that have turned into great sermon series. This book grew out of their experience at lunch one day at one of our favorite local dives, a small Mexican restaurant in Dayton, Taqueria Mixteca. The ideas were rolling out, and they sketched some notes on a napkin. This collaboration would not have happened without safety developed over time.

Trust:

Trust is the foundation of any healthy, well-functioning relationship, including a work or project-oriented team. Trust develops gradually. No matter the context of the relationship, trust is the result of consistency, dependability, increasing familiarity, honesty, and demonstrated integrity over time. While trust is built over time, it can be lost quickly. There is an old theory that still holds true as teams develop over time. Bruce Wayne Tuckman first published it in 1965 based on research around team dynamics. It became known as "Tuckman's Stages."

Author Shirley Lee describes the stages succinctly as follows:

Stage 1: Forming

The first stage is when the team is formed and members meet. They learn what the team opportunities and challenges will be. Individual members may be confused about their role or not understand the need for the team. Members will agree on goals and assign actions for work, often working independently. Ground rules or team guidelines are established. At the start, the team leader may be a member of the group, a supervisor, a manager, or a consultant who will facilitate the team-building process. Leadership will help the team to define their processes. At this stage, the leader needs to be directive and understand the requirements for team training to move through each stage.

Stage 2: Storming

During the second stage, individual expression of ideas occurs and there is open conflict between members. Members tend to focus on details rather than the issues and compete for influence. Low trust among team members is an evident indicator of this stage. The team needs to select their desired leadership style and decision methodology. The team leader can help by stressing tolerance and patience between members. The leader should guide the team process towards clear goals, defined roles, acceptable team behavior, and a mutual feedback process for team communication.

Stage 3: Norming

In the third stage, the team develops work habits that support group rules and values. They use established tools and methods and exhibit good behaviors. Mutual trust, motivation, and open communication increases. Additionally, positive teamwork and group focus are apparent. The team relationships grow and individual characteristics are understood and appropriately utilized. The team leader continues to encourage participation and professionalism among the team members.

Stage 4: Performing

The fourth stage shows high levels of loyalty, participation, motivation, and group decision-making. Knowledge sharing, cross-training, and interdependence increases. The team is self-directing in development of plans and strategy to meet their goals and carry out work. Personal growth and sharing are encouraged throughout membership. The leader becomes a facilitator aiding the team in communication processes and helping if they revert to a prior stage.

Stage 5: Adjourning

For project teams, temporary committees, or task forces coming to an end, there will be a finalizing stage as they celebrate and recognize group achievement. Then, some mourning over the dissolving of the team relationship and planning for the change in individual work requirements begins. During this stage, leadership needs to emphasize organization gratitude, including both team and individual recognition. For continuous work teams, there may be a higher performance level as they develop and transform as individuals and reform into revised teams. It is important to note that continuous work teams may revert to prior stages when new people are added to the team.

Time and effort are required to move through the various team development stages. Every team will go through all the stages. However, the timeline of each stage may be different for each team depending on the individual members, their skill levels, the work the team is expected to accomplish, and team leadership during each stage.[103]

Each one of Tuckerman's stages involves elements that are essential for teams to thrive. At every stage, teams must practice safety, trust, listening, giving permission, having a clear vision, and accountability. It is essential for the mission of the team. We love the way S. Truett Cathy, founder of Chick-fil-A, puts it: "We're not just in the chicken business,

---

[103] Lee, Shirley Fine. "The Team Building Directory." *The Team Building Directory Five Stages of Team Development Comments,* www.innovativeteambuilding.co.uk/five-stages-of-team-development/. Accessed December 9, 2019.

we're in the people business."[104] Cathy's words are a great reminder for the church seeking to be local. The church isn't merely a business, though business principles can be used. It's not about the most exciting marketing strategy, latest and greatest technology, rock bands, or eloquent speakers. At the end of the day, it's about people and our responsibility to shape people as disciples of Jesus Christ.

One image that may be helpful in thinking about what happens with trust in teams is what Jason calls the seesaw theory. The shorter a relationship has been in place, the shorter the seesaw board is, and the more susceptible it is to each person's movements. Misunderstandings and incidents that happen early in a relationship can destroy trust quickly - like one person slamming to the ground very quickly when the other pushes off the ground. The longer the relationship continues, the longer the seesaw board is, and incidents that might early on create dramatic shifts are less impactful as trust builds.

Listening:

Listening is a difficult art to master. Many of us are guilty of thinking about what we're going to say next instead of really listening to and absorbing someone else's ideas. When we don't listen, we can miss out on an important contribution from a team member. This often happens when people bring their own agendas to a meeting. A room full of agendas is a room in which everyone is waiting for their chance to talk, specifically to persuade the room toward their agenda. This will squash effective collaboration, especially when

[104] Dave Ramsey. *"7 Life Lessons from Truett Cathy." https://www.daveramsey.com/blog/7-life-lessons-from-truett-cathy.* Accessed December 18, 2019.

new ideas, new worship experiences, new ministries, or new campuses are being considered. If you are in a meeting and recognize that you have a room full of personal agendas, consider writing a purpose statement together to identify and clarify what the central agenda of the group is.

Roz has learned how important good listening is to successful mentorships. Some of the best mentors in his life have shown him what this looks like, and as a result, Roz has tried to practice good listening when he mentors younger people in ministry.

Much of mentoring isn't verbal coaching or lecturing. It's hearing what a mentee is going through and how they are processing their ministry experiences. If a mentor does all the talking, the relationship becomes one-sided. A mentor's job isn't to come up with all the best answers and solutions, but instead to guide a mentee through processing their circumstances on their own.

Another barrier to listening for Roz, and for many of us, when we're in creative meetings is that we get distracted easily. If Roz is on his phone or computer, it's impossible for him to listen well to others and fully participate in the creative process. Because he has noticed a dramatic difference in his own participation and listening skills, Roz puts his technology aside whenever possible and has a pen and paper ready instead.

Permission Giving:

The willingness to try new things and color outside the lines or boundaries of established practices or traditions requires our giving permission to our fellow collaborators. It's taking a risk to reach a prioritized goal. Without giving permission, it can become difficult to innovate. Permission-giving environments are low on enforcing control and high on setting expectations. These environments trust leaders and teams to get the job done and done well, but they don't dictate how to get the job done. There are very few restraints placed on team members. High-control and by-the-book companies and churches may be better suited to bringing managers on their teams instead of entrepreneurial leaders and thinkers. In the business world, franchisors don't give a high degree of permission to their franchisees for exploration. Local dives, on the other hand, have the advantage of experimentation in the kitchen in hopes of finding the right recipe and flavor for their customer base.

What could stop a group from achieving their mission? The question, "But, how?"

When asked too soon and too insistently we tend to (intentionally or unintentionally) demand conformity to the current practice.

Have you ever heard a fascinating premise put forth in a super-group setting, followed by thought-provoking back-and-forth, only to have the seed crushed by an untimely, "Yeah, but how?"

Don't get us wrong, it's important to have pragmatists around the table. But when you are in freethinking mode asking "How?" too soon can stop a brilliant idea right in its tracks. Innovation needs time to percolate. The mind needs time to see the possibilities and embrace a new reality. Forcing a new idea into the constraints of current reality and current practices closes the door on innovation. Creating a brainstorming atmosphere means throwing out the rulebook of expected methodologies and daring to be innovative.

On a related note, you may be a leader of a team because of your title or position. In the creative process, it's important to lead not by position but by example. Leadership should be more about function than it is position. Someone who doesn't have your role, qualifications, or experience may come up with a better idea, and it takes a healthy dose of humility to submit to the process and group.

As the Hollywood panelists pointed out, the best idea needs to win, regardless of who comes up with it. This is a great opportunity for leaders to keep their egos in check and empower those around them to succeed. If you lead out of your position of authority instead of out of a sense of humility, it can stifle the voices in the room. As the leader, make sure you're not doing all the talking. Try to create an even playing field where all the team members have permission to voice their ideas.

As a self-proclaimed war history buff, Roz can't help but draw from one of the great examples in history—that of Vice Admiral Horatio Nelson, who served in The Royal Navy for Great Britain in the late eighteenth century. Much has been written about Nelson's leadership, including the permission he gave to those who served under him.

A recent book written by General Stanley McChrystal (a retired four-star General in the U.S. Army), *Team of Teams: New Rules of Engagement for a Complex World*, describes what came to be known as "the Nelson touch." It's simple. When in battle, the Nelson touch is:

> *...the idea that individual commanders should act on their own initiative once the melee had developed. Noting that plans could be easily foiled, he gave a final, simple piece of advice: 'No captain can do very wrong if he places his ship alongside that of the enemy.' Nelson allowed his teammates to use their own critical thinking and initiative to carry out the mission because they had*

a clear vision of what the win was for them. The culture that was created long before the battle helped give permission to those who worked under Nelson. Nelson was the leader - no one had any doubt about that - but he was so confident in his own leadership that he was able to lead through teamwork instead of simply giving commands and lording his authority over the sailors.[105]

Reflection Questions:

Is your team thriving in the trust department, or struggling to find it? Are team members really listening to one another?

Have you established a "high control, low permission" environment or a "high permission, low control" environment?

How can you (or your leader) de-emphasize position and focus more on the function of leadership?

How can you ensure that the best idea wins?

Humility over pride:

Pride can easily occur when a team, church, organization, or leader experience some level of success. Leaders and organizations that are not careful can fall into the pride

[105] McCrystal, Stanley A., et al., "Sons of Proetus." *Team of Teams: New Rules of Engagement for a Complex World*, Portfolio/Penguin, 2015, p. 30.

trap. While the church debates what is sin and what is holy, there is one sin that has largely been ignored over the past few decades. It's subtle and starts out small, but can become uncontrollable. We're talking about the sin of pride resulting from success.

One of the most dangerous things a person can experience is success. Much is written about overcoming failure and setbacks, but we disregard the opposite. A glance at the available literature might lead us to the conclusion that success, especially success in ministry, has no pitfalls. It is the goal, after all. We don't set out in ministry to fail. The metrics the institutional church uses are butts and bucks: butts in seats to measure attendance, and bucks in giving that go toward the annual budget. The churches and clergy with the most butts and bucks are the ones who make the Top 25 lists and who are considered most influential. They receive awards and accolades. If you haven't discovered what we're referring to, attend a pastors' conference some time. Conversations center on attendance numbers and trends, annual budgets, and the size of staff and salaries.

Success itself is not the sin. The greatest danger of success is thinking you achieved it on your own. If we are not careful, pride can come before a fall. John Wesley, the founder of Methodism, believed that the root of all evil was pride. It was pride that caused Satan's fall from heaven because he thought he knew better than God. It was pride when Adam and Eve thought God was holding out on them in the Garden of Eden and that caused their fall. It was pride that caused the Tower of Babel to crash and burn. And it is pride that tempts us to think we have arrived on our own and leads us to sin.

In the Christian classic *Mere Christianity,* C.S. Lewis says:

> *According to Christian teachers, the essential vice, the utmost evil, is Pride. Unchastity, anger, greed,*

> *drunkenness, and all that, are mere flea bites in comparison: it was through Pride that the devil became the devil: Pride leads to every other vice: it is the complete anti-God state of mind ... it is Pride which has been the chief cause of misery in every nation and every family since the world began.*[106]

As a pastor, Roz humbly admits that he has experienced a ton of failures and a few "successes." When he fails, he turns to mentors and colleagues for counsel. They encourage him not to give up and talk him off the proverbial ledge. But nobody ever told him how to handle success, especially in ministry. More than anything, the world needs people and organizations grounded with a Christ-like humility. So how does Roz stay grounded, even in times of success? What follows are some points Roz has learned for remaining humble in the face of success.

First, Roz has learned to thank God when a prayer is answered and give glory to Him. There are so many times when God has answered a prayer, and Roz gets so excited he forgets to say "thank you." Roz's parents used to hound him to give thanks when he was growing up: always say "please" and "thank you!"

We are pretty good at saying "please," but when a prayer is answered, we thanklessly move to the next item on our grocery list. If we recognize that God has created us with a specific set of capabilities, that God has gifted us with specific ways we can bless others, that God has allowed us to be coworkers on Kingdom work and has given us specific missions and instructions to follow ... if we recognize all of

---

[106] Lewis, C. S. *Mere Christianity.* (New York: Simon & Schuster Touchstone edition, 1996), 109, 111.

this, we have to admit that the achievements that *look* like they were done by our own power really had very little to do with our "own" work and strengths to begin with! Thank God for allowing and enabling us to take part in His work!

Reflection Question:

Stop for a few minutes and say a prayer of thanks for all that God is currently doing in the midst of your ministry.

Second, Roz has learned the importance of thanking others. Whenever Roz's campus experiences a victory, he has learned to thank his paid and unpaid servants and staff. Without them, Roz knows he would be lost. Every team member is valuable, no matter their role or scope of responsibility. Again, we know that God brings people together at various times and in various settings, for God's specific purposes that we cannot fully comprehend or achieve on our own.

Although we may find ourselves with the title that says, "I'm the leader of this group," and while, sometimes, if we're completely honest, we may not even understand the contributions someone else is there to make, we must acknowledge and give thanks that God is the project manager and the casting director. Recognize those who work hard behind the scenes. As leaders, we can't say "thank you" enough to our teams, our support people, and even to the people who allow us to serve them.

God knows the plans God has for us. Plans to prosper us and not to harm us. Plans to bring us hope and a future. God *wants* our success, especially in those areas where God has gifted us, where God has placed us, and where God has directed and commissioned us. But God also wants others to see that—even as successful leaders—God's work is being done *through* us. We are not doing it alone! Even as the best of the best in whatever ministry we do, there's no miracle in doing human-sized tasks separate from God. When others see God working, God's work is accomplished. We can help others see God's work by remaining humble and thankful in our moments of success.

Third, Roz has learned to be thankful for those who will tell him the truth. When an individual, organization, or church experiences success, the resulting pride of the leadership can make it hard for others to ask tough questions, for others to be willing to tell us the truth, and for us to hear the truth. Roz knows who the people are in his life who love him the most and are willing to be honest with him.

Of course, trust has to be at the foundation. If you trust where someone is coming from and know they care about you, the truth in what they are saying may still sting in the short term, but it will soothe your soul in the long run. Many voices in the Church seek to be "prophetic," but they don't bring the truth with love. Truth-tellers come in the context of relationship.

Fourth, Roz has learned the importance of practicing affirmation. People often hear about the mistakes they made and not the times they have done a good job. It's imperative to give your team affirmation. One person can set the tone, and it can become contagious. Affirmation can go a long way. It is recognition for a job well done, but also honoring the person publicly or privately to show appreciation. Saddleback Church Pastor Rick Warren gives four tangible ways for communicating affirmation.

First, Warren encourages us to *value each other's ideas.*

There is no such thing as a dumb idea. Even if teammates have a differing opinion or philosophy, when you value people's opinions, they will continue to offer them. When we shut people out or down, they will be reluctant to speak up the next time. Valuing each other's ideas communicates that everybody is unique and equal.

Second, Warren says to *appreciate uniqueness*. When a team is diverse, it's important to acknowledge other perspectives. When we appreciate a person, we communicate to them and to the team as a whole that they are uniquely made by God. This also creates space for an ever-expanding army. Team members can be added with little or no threat to the individuals on the team. Every person becomes a gift.

Third, Warren tells us to *commend efforts*. If we are in the people business, we should acknowledge the hard work people put in, even when the results aren't what we expect. Individuals can work as hard as possible with the right strategy, but ultimately God brings the fruit of the labor. There are times we don't see that fruit immediately. When we commend people's efforts, we are telling them that we see them and their work. They will continue to put effort into the mission and each other in relationships.

Last, Warren encourages us to *praise loyalty*. It's rare nowadays for people to stick with the same job in the secular world, and it's no different in a church. When we celebrate and praise the dedication of teammates, it expresses that you want them to still be around. When we forget to praise loyalty, it can send an unintended message that they are replaceable.[107]

---

[107] Warren, Rick. "8 Values of TEAMWORK That Keep a Church Healthy." www.Pastors.com, pastors.com/8-values-of-teamwork-that-keep-a-church-healthy/, 27 Mar. 2015.

Clear Vision:

Everybody's aim should be on the same target. It's hard to hit a moving target or a target with ill-defined lines. If team members don't know the desired outcome, the method for getting there is completely arbitrary. On the other hand, anyone who has had the chance to work with a group of like-minded individuals knows how inspiring it is to work together toward a shared vision. This doesn't mean the group is composed of similar people.

For example, Roz's worship design team at Mosaic Church is made up of two pastors, a full-time caregiver, a schoolteacher who works with students with special needs, and a high school art teacher. Each team member is valuable and brings unique insight to the creative process.

While the team is diverse, when it comes to the mission at hand, the group is on the same page and freed up to take necessary steps toward fulfilling the mission. You can have the best and brightest in the room, but if they don't have a common vision or goal for a project, it is a complete waste of time.

Have you ever left a meeting wondering what the purpose or desired outcome was? This can be a clear indication that there was little vision in the first place. The meeting time is the place to define team visions.

Roz recalls that he wasn't a college basketball fan until his early twenties when he moved to the Bluegrass state. He quickly learned that Kentucky takes three things very seriously: horses, bourbon, and the University of Kentucky Wildcats basketball.

Roz saw firsthand the enthusiasm for the Wildcats when, in 2012, he witnessed pandemonium break out in the streets as drunken college students burned living room couches in celebration of a victory.

A common criticism of the coach is that his players use college basketball as a stepping stone to the NBA and don't stay long on the UK team. However, the players he attracts are known not only for their individual accomplishments, but also for their impressive commitment to the team's vision. Case in point, the 2012 UK team had gone 31-0 in the regular season, and yet, the only player from UK who made the top fifteen Wooden finalists, Willie Cauley-Stein, a phenomenal player, averaged fewer than ten points per game. This is without a doubt one of the most selfless college basketball teams in history. They are so selfless that only two of their players averaged double-digit points per game (Aaron Harrison 11.2 and Devin Booker 10.9). Many of the players in recent years could be stars on any other NCAA team, but they care more about the team winning than individual stats and accolades.

What if the Church was more selfless in "giving away" the ministry to all people? What if pastors shared their pulpit more? What if other members of the team were celebrated and invested in, even if that means the leader doesn't get the credit? What if those in leadership positions try constantly to replace themselves so that others become mature disciples, ready to lead? What if we were less focused on job security and personal accolades, and more focused on our shared vision of the Kingdom being advanced? What if that meant churches working together across denominational lines to reach a city? Sounds a lot like a food truck rally! Call us crazy, but we believe it's possible. We've even seen it happen.

Some of the best teams we've worked with have been so focused on advancing the Kingdom that no one can remember who proposed that great idea that brought new people to the church. When Roz was in urban ministry, some of the most Kingdom-minded churches he's worked with have said, "We might have the resources and be Baptist while you are Methodist, but you are in the neighborhood where lost and hurting people need the gospel, and we want to partner even if those people ultimately end up at your church because they can walk there and not to our own." It's rare, but it's possible.

Accountability:

Team members carry out their duties and do what they say they will do. If a meeting ends and action steps are not articulated, nothing is going to be accomplished. Accountability is saying, "Give me the next thing to do," and doing it. Follow-through is crucial after any creative meeting or session. It is necessary to have clear action steps following any session where there are a lot of ideas floating around. Accountability will refine the goal and move everyone toward it with a timeline in mind. Without accountability deadlines are missed, goals are not accomplished, and time is wasted. Some teams fall in love with the process so much that they fail to put expectations in place. This is a delicate balance. Process is important but it's not more important than the results.

Celebrate the wins:

Churches are notorious for completing one major task or initiative or having a successful event and moving on to the next thing. At Mosaic Church, Roz's team has tried to immediately celebrate successes. They do simple things like treat everybody for ice cream after a major event, or scrap a regularly scheduled meeting and go out for dinner or an outing.

When we fail to celebrate wins, we are taking people on the team for granted and forgetting to give glory to God. Also, when we don't acknowledge accomplishments but keep piling on the work, we can end up with teams and individuals who are burned out.

When all these elements are in place, we can make an irresistible meal together. Have you experienced this type of high-functioning group? The Church needs a local dive that empowers all Christians to do ministry work, without creating silos led by staff.

Reflection Questions:

How can you intentionally and proactively give thanks for and affirm those around you?

Do you have people around you who can tell you the truth and hold you accountable?

Have you recently worked on and communicated your vision?

CHAPTER 7
WORTH THE WAIT
ESSENTIAL INGREDIENTS

When it comes to great food (and great worship), people will line up and wait for long periods of time to take part in it. People waited six hours to hear Ezra's preaching. His team was at the ready to translate the Word for the people. Ezra's message and his delivery of it were worth the wait, and those gathered were moved deeply by it.

In a time when church attendance is on the decline, let's look at successful churches that have lines at the door. Jason was recently invited to co-lead an immersive retreat designed to help churches improve their guest readiness and first impression teams.

The retreat took place in Charlotte, North Carolina, and included visits to three area churches. One of the visits was to Elevation Church, which is led by Pastor Steven Furtick. Upon approaching the church, signs can be seen up and down the road inviting first time visitors to turn on their hazard lights. This allows the hospitality teams to direct first-time guests to the visitor parking lot. Yes, they have an entire lot designated for first time visitors.

As Jason and the group pulled into the visitor lot, he was taken aback when he saw that the lot was nearly full. The lot for regular attendees was equally packed. A line of people wrapped around the building, everyone patiently waiting to participate in the evening's worship service. Teams of volunteers were strategically placed to tend to any needs or questions worshipers might have.

As first-time guests, Jason and the other participants were treated as VIPs. Extra special hospitality was extended. The group was offered a place closer to the front of the line, and some of the best seats in the house were made available to them. The excitement of those gathered was incredible.

Elevation's worship is rooted in dynamic preaching, the

highest quality of music, top-notch media and visuals, all set in a modern facility that could easily host The Grammys.

The recipe that Elevation has developed is resonating so deeply with its local community that it has grown many times larger than its original campus, making it one of the best-known multi-site megachurches in the country. A key factor in its growth is its inviting, appealing style and the teams that support its ministry.

What we cook up in the kitchen must whet the appetites of the people who live here and now. It's important to note that the recipe for worship that each and every one of us fell in love with was an acquired taste. We grew to love it over time.

Too often, when we resist changing the recipe for worship, it's because we're confusing the context in which we encountered Jesus with the Gospel itself. Jason's old ministry partner and Texas native Len Wilson used to say, "We confuse Jesus and the horse He road in on in our lives." We tend to treat context as sacred, which is why many of us are still preparing recipes that are outdated and unattractive.

When was the last time you had a line of people waiting to attend worship? Let's be honest—when was the last time *you* were truly excited about the recipe you're serving up in worship? Truth is, far too many of us aren't even moved by the worship offered at our own churches. If our worship doesn't move us, we can't expect others to stand in line for it either.

In this chapter, we want to explore what it takes to make a meal worth the wait—a meal that will keep people coming back.

Creativity, imagination, and innovation are essential ingredients of creating a winning recipe. Might we once again strive to create worship that has a sense of mystery and intrigue? Could we also find a way to create worship worth lining up for? We believe the answer is yes.

During the downturn in the economy in 2008, many restaurants struggled and shut down, giving rise to the food truck. A food truck can prepare a meal with local flavor cheaply and accessibly. Have you seen the lines behind these beloved restaurants on wheels?

In some parts of the country, food trucks are so popular that they are restricted from setting up shop too close to brick and mortar restaurants, so as to protect the established restaurants. A nimble food truck operator who can change recipes and develop specialties from one day to the next threatens established franchises with more red tape in their kitchens. Additionally, restaurants often have to maintain a broader menu in order to be profitable. Due to space constraints, food trucks specialize. They find their niche, perfect it, and tweak as they go. The give and take between chef and consumer is also different. Food truck customers often dig in to their food immediately after it is handed to them, in close proximity to the person who prepared it. At most restaurants, on the other hand, the cooks stay in the kitchen and rarely hear feedback firsthand, or see the look on a person's face as they take that first bite.

As local churches, we must also identify and offer specialties to our communities. Rather than attempt to be a little bit of everything to everyone, we must make hard choices to focus our resources on the things that will have the most impact in our communities.

What is unique about your community? What are its greatest strengths and its greatest needs? What resources do you have to meet the unique needs where you serve?

While there are multiple considerations in making a winning recipe for your new endeavor, we believe there are five key ingredients required for making a recipe that people will come back for. These are:

1. **Worship**
2. **Guest Readiness**
3. **Community Building**
4. **Discipleship**
5. **Mission**

Worship

We have coached church planters over the years who become so wrapped up in the details of establishing a new faith community, that creating great worship is an afterthought. It's easy to understand how this happens. You have to acquire space, worry about branding, create a budget, buy equipment, build a launch team, and the list goes on.

These details are vital, but if you get everything in place, then serve a half-baked recipe for worship, all the hours of planning can be ruined very quickly. It's never too early in the process to craft deep, meaningful worship.

No matter what style of worship you plan to offer, there are essential elements to consider.

1. Environment

The local dive you hope to create could be starting a whole new faith community, starting a new campus, or moving to a new location. It could also just be creating a new worship experience that is different from what is already established at your church. Maybe you're doing something new in an old space. Perhaps your new service is taking place in a traditional sanctuary, a gymnasium, a fellowship hall, or a chapel.

Whatever the new endeavor, the environment matters. Holding "modern" or "contemporary" worship in a traditional space can be problematic if the music, preaching, and liturgy don't fit the vibe of the room. Worshiping in a gymnasium with no acoustical treatment can be equally bad, and the space might feel so massive that even a large crowd would feel swallowed up.

Depending on your situation, you may have the ability to permanently renovate a space to fit the vibe of your intended worship style, or you may be forced to reset the room between services and do what you can to make it feel different. If you're reusing a shared space that cannot be permanently altered, what can you do to differentiate it for the new recipe you plan to offer?

Lighting changes are a great start to making the room feel different from something that already exists. Colored lights, gobos, and patterns projected on walls, fabrics, and backdrops, can enhance a space and change its look.

Environmental projection - pointing projectors at walls and other surfaces - is a wonderful way to make a space feel unique. Environmental projection can transform just about any space into something special. Imagine telling the story of Jesus walking on water and seeing storms projected on the walls behind a storyteller. Or maybe you are doing a series on mountaintop experiences, and you turn the stage into a base camp with physical tents, bags, and chairs, and project a mountain scene behind the props. The creative possibilities are endless. Cameron Ware originated this practice back in the mid-2000s.[108] Check out his site, www.visualworshiper.com, for examples.

---

108 www.Visualworshiper.com.

You might also incorporate creative elements connected to your series into the space. Visuals can range from abstract and eye-catching, to more tangible displays, and even fully constructed sets. A few favorites we've seen over the years include:

- A large stack of white cardboard boxes, pushed out at different angles, with colored light shone on them.
- Strings of square Styrofoam paper plates affixed to the wall, with colored light shone on them.
- A recreation of the set from Mr. Rogers' Neighborhood for a series about being a good neighbor.
- A five-gallon bucket painted yellow with a label attached to look like a giant Play-Doh container.
- A collection of random bags (backpack, computer bag, laundry bags) for a series about letting God carry our baggage.
- A collection of doors (metal, wood, screen, etc.) at the front of the worship space for a series about Jesus knocking at the doors of our hearts.

The look of your worship space matters and should be given as much attention as branding and communications. It is easy for the recipe for the look of worship to get stale quickly, so consider changing it up every series or, at the very least, a few times a year.

2. Music

Choosing the right style of music for your local dive is among the highest of priorities. The assumption might be that if you're starting something new, you have to go with the latest cutting-edge music style. But this is not always the case.

As with every other consideration, local context matters more than copying someone else's sound and feel. Not every music style is going to work in every location. Your local dive might thrive with a folksy sound. It may be best with a K-LOVE vibe. You may end up with the best country and western worship experience ever concocted. The music needs to be about you, your community, and the team available to you.

Jason was recently in Topeka, Kansas, to lead a seminar for the Great Plains Conference of the United Methodist Church. The leaders asked him to collaborate with one of their up-and-coming pastors, Chris Aytes, to design a worship experience. It was decided that Jason would provide the creative elements, spoken word, and sermon, while Chris and his band would provide the music leadership. The music portion of the worship was so unique and powerful, Jason had to know more about its origins and the impact it was having on Chris' church. Chris sat down with Jason to tell the story.[109]

WAMEGO UMC, WAMEGO, KS

Chris is the associate pastor of Wamego United Methodist

[109] Interview with Chris Aytes, Nov 19, 2019.

Church—a church that, after a season of decline is once again thriving. Prior to Chris' arrival, Wamego had two traditional services that were fairly stagnant and steadily shrinking in weekly attendance. A handful of musicians in the church would occasionally come together to lead the church in a more contemporary style. When a new lead pastor, Michael Tomson-DeGreeff, was appointed to the church, he began searching for a bandleader to set up a new, non-traditional service.

A year later, pastor Chris was brought on board. Within a of couple years, the contemporary service had doubled in size, in part because of Pastor Chris and his band's unique and ultra-contextual music style.

Chris describes it like this: "Our music is kind of a Johnny Cash, 1950's rockabilly/Sun Studios vibe. Think early rock-and-roll meets country." He explains that they were regularly experimenting, and two key factors ultimately shaped their sound.

First, Chris had spent about ten years playing in bars, coffee shops, and local dives near the church. He had to find his own sound before he could bring something unique to the church, and this time allowed him to learn who he was as a musician. Those years of gigging taught Chris valuable lessons.

When Chris became the bandleader, rather than copying the sounds of other artists' recordings, he relied on personal expression. He strove to interpret popular worship music into a recipe that fit his band's musical prowess and the tastes of the congregation. Chris believes this authenticity and playing to one's strengths makes great worship music. "Finding your sound is so important. What did God create you to sound like? Sound like that, not someone else."

Chris points to Joe Cocker's hit remake of the Beatles song, "With A Little Help from My Friends." "Joe made that song his own thing using his own style and it was brilliant. The audacity of taking a Beatles' song and remaking it was a risk that might have seemed absurd at the time. Of course, it found an audience with people who may or may not have liked the Fab Four. By many accounts, it may be [Cocker's] most recognized tune."

In the same way Cocker brought his unique sound to the original material, Chris found out what sound would make the most sense for the musicians he'd be working with. He even conducted a survey of his band, asking them what type of music they liked, listened to, and enjoyed playing most. This helped Chris understand the ingredients available for forming a unique sound that would resonate.

Chris took what he had learned about adapting popular music for bar and club shows and applied it to worship music. One particular weekend, Chris said, "When we did the arrangement for "I Have Decided to Follow Jesus," I noticed that the melody and the chord progression felt a lot like something Johnny Cash would do. We leaned into it, adapting the hymn to the point that it sounded like a cut from *At Folsom Prison*. The first time we played it in worship, the congregation erupted into an explosion of genuine applause and excitement. It was unlike anything we'd seen before. We knew we had something that morning."

The more they experimented with this style of music, the more they found that it resonated with their surrounding community in Midwest Kansas. "For us and where we live, we came to the realization that this music scratches the itch for multiple generations. The eldest members of our congregation grew up on that early rock-n-roll, and they raised their kids on it as well. This music, in our context, has been passed on from generation to generation and has a sort of universal appeal."

Again, context is so important. Chris says, "If I was

serving a church full of young hipsters in Brooklyn, I'd probably be playing an entirely different style of music. Our band has the chops to play lots of different styles, but this rockabilly style we're known for really connects deeply with our people. Once you know who you are, you can bend a song to fit your audience."

Another crucial piece for selecting worship music is your church's "why." Years ago, Jason consulted with a church who had plateaued in attendance and wanted to reformulate their recipe. The church offered several worship experiences: two "high church" traditional services, a millennial-focused contemporary service, and a boomer-oriented contemporary service.

The boomer-oriented service was the best attended. While they called this service their "blue jeans" service, Jason lovingly referred to it as the "Peter, Paul, and Mary" service. The music was folksy with a 1980s or 1990s feel to the worship order. Meanwhile, the millennial service was the newest and least attended service. It had a more casual worship order and vibe.

The leader of the boomer-oriented service lamented to Jason that they'd been trying to reach young people and were striking out. When he asked Jason how he would suggest they reach more millennials, Jason's response was, "Why? This is your biggest service. It's meeting a need. And you have a millennial focused service already, so why would you try and reach that target here, too?"

Jason encouraged the church to embrace their strengths. Rather than trying to force musicians who were thriving in folk music into a mold to attract millennials, instead to celebrate, perfect, and promote their team's sweet spot. Chances are pretty good that would not have experienced much success outside that sweet spot anyway.

3. Theme Setup (Liturgy)

Another aspect of worship that can set apart a new recipe from an old one is in the way themes and narratives play out over multiple elements in the same service. In older, more established liturgies, it's very easy for the pieces to come off as disconnected, like in a pageant of unrelated acts performing in succession. The acts can vary wildly from one to the next and usually have no narrative thread. Take for instance *America's Got Talent*, a modern-day pageant show. One recent episode's guests included a ventriloquist, an acrobat, and a singing group. Each act performed their talent, moving from one random act to the next.

Worship, whether traditional or contemporary, can feel the same. When the theme hasn't been intentionally tied to other elements, the pieces feel disjointed, confusing, and worship can ultimately lose its meaning. Worship might begin with a time of singing, followed by the welcome or announcements. The welcome and announcements may have no connection to any of the songs sung just moments before. From there, worship may move into scripture and prayer. Again, the scripture may be unrelated to the songs, the welcome, or the announcements. Worship may become even more incohesive with a moment meant for children that may not tie back to the scripture, the songs, or the adult sermon that will follow moments later. We've even experienced worship where the sermon doesn't relate to the scripture that was read earlier, because the reading came from a common lectionary that the pastor is not preaching on that day.

Instead, if a theme is established early and carried through all elements of worship, the message makes sense from the beginning and is reinforced throughout. This narrative form of worship leaves the worshiper with one big idea reinforced over and over, rather than four or five disparate ideas that are easily forgotten. Many years ago at Ginghamsburg Church, Pastor Michael Slaughter used to say that it was the team's job to put him on the one-yard line so that all he had to do was trip to score a touchdown.

When a theme is properly set up and carried through all of the elements, people hunger for the message at the end. Think of it as a story with each chapter written in concert with one another. A theme ties the scripture to the title, metaphor, or image for the series or standalone message. This should ideally be done early in worship so that images on the screen or print piece make sense right away.

Here's an example from a recent series based on John 15:9-13 using a domino metaphor. The series title was *Set in Motion:*

Good morning! Let me ask you a question this morning. By a show of hands, how many of you have played the game dominoes? How many of you are like me, and you've spent less time playing the game than you have lining those little chunks of wood or plastic up into intricate patterns, only to push the first one down and waiting to see if your creation makes it all the way to completion? Any of you do that?

For a domino rally to complete, there are three things that need to take place. 1) The dominoes have to be in alignment with each other – one domino out of place and the momentum stops dead in its tracks. 2) The dominoes have to be in close proximity with one another – too much space between the dominoes, and the momentum stops dead in it tracks. And finally, 3) an outside force has to set it all in motion.

This morning our scripture comes from John 15:9-13, and we find Jesus meeting with his disciples, teaching them some important lessons they might implement to live into what he's called them to.

He says to them, "As the Father has loved me, so I love you. Remain in my love."

It is in those words that we see God's domino effect playing out before us. The love of the Father passes to the son; then to the disciples; to the world; throughout time; to someone else's life that had an impact on you. And now it comes to us.

Will we be a continuation of God's movement and knock down the dominoes around us?

Let us stand and worship the God who ***Set It All in Motion.***

A theme setup like this (or a "call to worship" as it is known in more traditional settings) does an excellent job of setting the table and helps everyone understand the narrative thrust of the experience ahead.

4. Media Integration

We live in an increasingly visual society. Another essential element that should be included in our local dive recipes for worship is the use of images and rich visuals.

Research over the years confirms that the majority of people in our culture are visual learners. In fact, about 65% of us tend to be visual learners.[110] Additionally, studies show

[110] Gutierrez, Karla. ShiftLearning.com. "Studies Confirm the Power of Visuals in e-Learning." https://www.shiftelearning.com/blog/bid/350326/studies-confirm-the-power-of-visuals-in-elearning. July 8, 2014.

that learning increases by up to 400% when visuals are used to communicate and teach. Did you know that 70% of your sensory receptors are in your eyes?[111]

These realities are certainly reflected in the current social media landscape. In recent years the usership of Twitter (a medium focused on text) has declined, while the usership of Instagram (a medium focused on images) has dramatically increased.

Of course, improperly used images can detract from learning as well. The phrase "a picture is worth a thousand words" rings true for those who are looking for meaning. If those 1,000 words have nothing to do with the big ideas being explored in a sermon or a set of songs, we may do more harm than good. If we're not intentional, our images can be nothing more than out-of-sync eye candy that ultimately decreases the effectiveness of our messaging.

Karla Gutierrez of Shift Learning puts it like this: "It is important to note that graphics can also negatively impact learning if they are used inappropriately. When off-topic graphics appear on the screen, such as those used for purely decorative purposes, learners will subconsciously try to figure out the message and reason for the image."[112]

So how does this impact the worship experiences we create? Consistency is extremely important in the images and icons we use in worship. This is true for everything from the print pieces (the bulletin, the program, the worship folder, etc.) to the screen, and everything in between. The images on the stage or chancel, the displays leading into the worship

---

[111] https://neomam.com/interactive/13reasons/. Accessed December 18, 2019.

[112] Gutierrez, Karla. ShiftLearning.com. "Studies Confirm the Power of Visuals in eLearning." https://www.shiftelearning.com/blog/bid/350326/studies-confirm-the-power-of-visuals-in-elearning. Accessed December 9, 2019.

space, everything a worshiper sees—it all matters.

For example, when a title or series theme is presented, veering from it during the time of singing to display an entirely different image or visual style can undo the work you've put into establishing the day's concept.

Rather than matching images to song lyrics, or just using abstract backgrounds or nature footage behind the musicians, a consistent visual metaphor connected to the big idea will keep the narrative thread running throughout.

For instance, in the ***Set in Motion*** theme described above, after having established the metaphor and title of the domino effect, it would be a step backward to display images of oceans, stars, or wheat fields on screen behind the song lyrics. An image of dominoes is equally easy to find and will maintain focus on the theme, even if only on a subconscious level. If you are going to use abstract motion backgrounds, at least consider using the same color scheme and/or visual treatment that is congruent with the main graphics package being throughout the rest of the worship experience.

These concepts apply to social media and print as well. Use the same images and metaphors that you have created for your bulletin/program/worship folder on your Facebook page, Instagram account, TikTok, and other mediums.

It is worth noting that visuals are not meant to replace auditory, tactile, and text-based learning. All forms of learning are important and valid, and all elements should come together to reinforce a common theme.

5. Message Tie-In

Creativity in worship is only as good as its ability to convey meaning in the moment and after. Tying the message into the creativity playing out throughout worship is essential. Many churches retooling their worship recipes unintentionally fall into the trap of planning excellent metaphor or theme-based worship, only to have it all fall apart during the sermon.

The narratives can be set up in the spoken word and carried through the music, media, prayers, and tactile experiences. Then, when the sermon shows up, it's as if the theme vanishes. Preachers who don't understand and embrace the power of the narrative thread may offer a quick throwaway line at the top of the sermon, then continue on their way using their standard homiletical approach.

We cannot overstate the importance of redeeming the metaphor in the sermon. It's the pastor's role to exegete (interpret) not only the scripture, but also the metaphorical narrative (series branding) so that only the gospel shines through it, rather than being covered up by it. Creativity can obstruct the good news when bridges aren't built between the metaphor and the message. A sermon's language has to be tweaked, "wordsmithed," and tied into the visuals and narratives present in the rest of the service. Failing to do so can create confusion.

Several years ago, Jason was worshiping at a large church on Easter morning. The church had pulled out all the stops for this big day, adding additional lights, projections, and other creative elements to its worship space. Projected on the back wall, 20 feet wide by 20 feet tall was the title of this creative worship experience. (To protect the anonymity of this church, we won't share the title.) Many times throughout worship, these words were spoken by worship hosts, worship leaders, and in pre-recorded videos. They were printed on the bulletin, banners, and signs installed on the front lawn.

When the pastor got up to preach, he never once uttered the title of this experience. He never picked up on the themes, narratives, or metaphors. By comparison, the sermon felt "off topic" from everything that preceded it.

At the conclusion of worship, the pastor approached Jason in search of constructive feedback. Jason responded by saying, "Pastor, the movie *Captain America and the Winter Soldier* is out in theaters. Can you imagine buying a ticket to that film, settling into your seat with popcorn and cola, and watching a film where the Winter Soldier never shows up? Can you imagine how odd it would be if the story never mentioned or included this character in the plot? That's what I felt this morning as I sat in worship. There was a buildup throughout the experience, and then it was never tied into the sermon." The coachable pastor made adjustments to his sermons for the following services, extending the narrative throughout, which improved the entire experience.

The work of exegeting the metaphor happens through stories, sermon points, and intentional language. For instance, in the ***Set in Motion*** sermon based on John 15 ("As the father loves me, so I love you, remain in my love"), the sermon points explore three key ideas.

POINT ONE

Alignment – In the passage, Jesus tells the disciples that remaining in His love means obeying His commands. In doing this His joy will be in them and their joy will be complete.

When it comes to building domino rallies, the dominoes have to be aligned so that the momentum transfers from one to another. There's certainly a lot of joy in seeing that happen.

POINT TWO

Proximity – In the passage, Jesus talks about the sacrifice involved in loving one's friends enough to lay one's life down for them. Sacrifice can mean getting close enough to lean in to the people.

In the same way, with a domino rally, the dominoes have to be close enough to one another to continue the momentum.

POINT THREE

Set in Motion – Earlier in John 14, Jesus tells the disciples that if they believe in him, they will do works like he's done and even greater. When it comes to dominoes, one domino starts something that sets off a chain reaction of great things.

Jesus set this all in motion. Later in John 15, he shows them the whole progression – from the Father, to the Son, into the disciples, and so on.

Another aspect of the sermon covers the power of the Holy Spirit that is within each of us. Using the image of two dominoes, the preacher talks about the shift from potential energy (stored energy) to kinetic energy (energy in motion). The final story in the sermon illustrates the domino effect in a different way. [113]

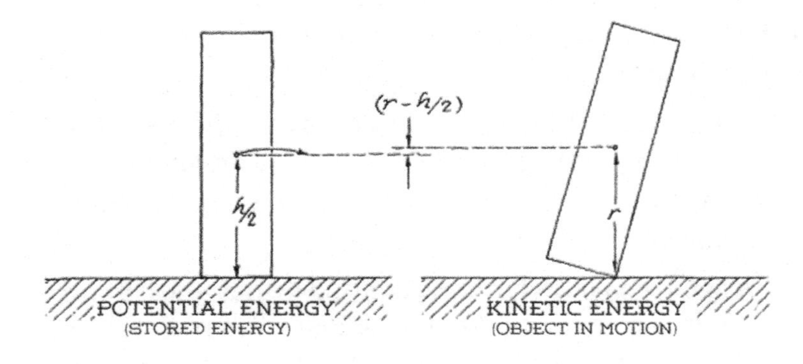

It begins by telling the story of Edward Kimball, who agrees to teach a Sunday school class. Edward learns many years later that one of his star students, a young man named Dwight, credits a conversation with him as the moment

[113] Featherstone, Jennifer. TheStoryofLibertyBlog.com. "Edward Kimball to Billy Graham an Amazing Timeline of Events." https://thestoryoflibertyblog.com/2012/06/18/edward-kimball-to-billy-graham-an-amazing-timeline-of-events/. Accessed December 9, 2019.

where his faith was activated. This Dwight just happened to be Dwight L. Moody, one of the great leaders of the church. Dwight's story continues as he later gives counsel to a man named J. Wilbur Chapman. Chapman walks away transformed in his ministry and goes on to employ a young preacher named Billy Sunday. Sunday influenced many with his mastery of the early medium of radio. One of his listeners, Mordecai Ham, came to faith in part because of Billy's ministry. Ham's call took him from city to city as a tent revivalist, preaching the good news everywhere he went. One night, on a stop in North Carolina, a young man was so inspired by what he heard that he was led to Christ. This man was Billy Graham. The dominoes that fell and continue to fall over the course of Graham's ministry are too numerous to count.

Edward Kimball could never have known how his sacrifice of obedience would lead to such great things. This story is tied closely to the image of the dominoes, including the way it was illustrated graphically on the screen. As you create your new recipe, be sure to leave room to tie the message to the creative narratives.

6. Missional Application

The last essential element to consider when it comes to worship is missional application. A key question we should be asking is how we can reframe our thinking about worship to make it the front door to discipleship and missional action in the world. Too often we approach worship design more theoretically than practically. We ask "what if" questions, rather than offering "here's how" opportunities.

As Jesus followers, we don't get to experience the fullness of our faith until we put it into practice. We do our congregations a disservice when we fail to give them specific opportunities to live their faith through missional action. The new recipe for worship should be action-oriented. This means that missional components are planned in and alongside worship.

When worship planners exegete both the scripture and the metaphor, missional opportunities arise with ease. During one series entitled "Baggage Check" at Roz's church, the narrative thrust centered on Matthew 11:28, "Come to me, all you that labor and are heavy laden, and I will give you rest" (ESV). The series offered worshipers the opportunity to allow God to take their burdens and carry them. During the sermon, Roz pulled items out of a bag that represented the heavy things he had carried throughout his life. One week during the series, people were invited to write a personal burden on a "bag check" tag, anything they were ready to let God carry for them. The tags were brought forward and placed into a suitcase during a time of interactive prayer.

MOSAIC CHURCH, BAGGAGE CHECK SERIES

The missional application was presented in a challenge to the congregation to collect backpacks and school supplies for local schools with high populations of underprivileged kids. The impact this had on the church and community was incredible, and the offering largely happened in worship, rather than as an outside project.

Another example comes from work Jason did at Grace United Methodist Church in Piqua, Ohio. In conjunction with World Communion Sunday, Jason and the team at Grace began brainstorming about how to help people see God in new ways. With the Lord's Supper as the foundation, the team found inspiration in the idea that Jesus gives us the tools to see Him every day in the daily meal. When He tells the disciples, "When you eat this bread and drink this cup, do so in remembrance of me," the power of the visual image isn't meant just for that moment, but extends to us even today.

The series was entitled "Believing is Seeing" and featured the image of a peanut butter and jelly sandwich. As the team worked, Jason remembered a friend of his, Jerry Herships, who had been making peanut butter and jelly sandwiches in worship for years to hand out to the homeless.

The idea was floated to the team, and everyone became excited about doing something similar at Grace. Over the course of four weeks, the congregation was invited to bring in jars of peanut butter, jelly, bread, and sides to be assembled in the third week of the series.

On the Friday before the assembly week, doorhangers were made and distributed to some of the poorest neighborhoods in their city. The note explained that on Sunday, the church would be back in the neighborhood to offer bag lunches. Households that wanted to participate could hang the door-hangers on their doors so that the church knew where to stop.

On that Sunday morning, during worship, and as an act of worship, the congregation moved to tables to make sandwiches and fill brown bags with sandwiches and sides. In a very short period of time, accompanied by a time of singing, the church assembled over 360 bag lunches. Following worship, congregants packed into vehicles and delivered meals to the neighborhoods. The group of volunteers from the church was so large that it only took about fifteen minutes to distribute all the lunches.

Story after story of gratitude were shared from the various households they had visited. One single mother answered the door in disbelief saying that she'd just prayed ten minutes prior that God would help her feed her kids that day.

At Mosaic Church, Roz and his team created a series called "Spin Cycle" which used images and the metaphor of the washing machine to explore the process by which God forgives us and makes us whole. The missional opportunity they dreamed up was to hand out small detergent bottles and instructional cards inviting people to a laundromat in the area where the church would pay for their laundry to be washed.

Finally, another series Jason was a part of entitled "Half Full" used a glass of water that was half full/empty to describe what a lifestyle filled with the Spirit looked like. Congregants were challenged to bring bottled water every week of the series to be distributed to a homeless shelter at the completion of the series.

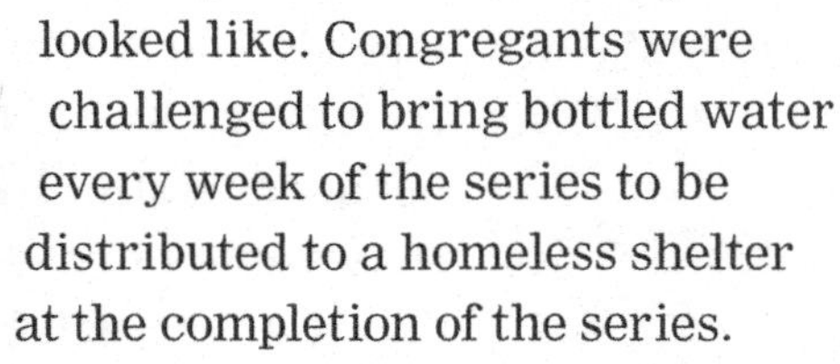

Moving toward action might mean one other major shift in the recipe you create for worship. The way you get people to engage in mission matters, so we have one radical idea for you to consider: stop doing announcements! That's right—discontinue the practice of sharing three or four random pieces of information at the beginning of worship, and instead make them action steps, tied to the sermon, at the end.

There are a few reasons announcements don't work. First, they feel random and disconnected from the narrative. Second, they're often done first thing and are followed by a time of reading scripture, prayer, other elements, and a sermon. Forty-five to fifty minutes later, people can't remember what you said and therefore don't sign up. Third, they feel redundant because, in many settings, the announcements are included on a piece of paper in the bulletin. And last, there's no way to sign up for what's being announced at that moment.

Here's what a typical announcement set might look like in worship:

> *Good morning friends! I'd like to tell you some of the things happening in the life of our church. First, summer camp is coming up soon, and we'd like to help as many kids from our church go as possible. Some of you are culinary artists and can make incredible desserts. We'd like to have a bake sale to raise money to help send our kids to camp. Can you help us with that? We hope so.*
>
> *Next, some of you may have heard that there was a fire in one of the homes in our community. The family has lost so much. Habitat for Humanity is working to rebuild their home, and our church is putting together a crew to help in the reconstruction effort. We'd love to see you there.*
>
> *Finally, our women's ministry is meeting on Tuesday night for their monthly gathering. This is a wonderful*

time of sharing in friendship, food, and faith. If you're a lady (sorry guys), we hope you'll consider joining them at 6:00 pm in the youth room.

As stated, this information, while valuable, has no narrative thread, feels random, and there's no real way to act in the moment. Here's what that same information looks like as action steps using the *Set in Motion* theme after the sermon:

Friends, we've just spent the past hour exploring what God's domino effect in the world looks like. Don't you want to be a part of that momentum as we move into the week? I'd like to share three opportunities to set your faith in motion this week.

First, some of the dominoes we hope to impact in our church are our young people. Summer camp will be here soon, and we hope to raise money to fuel God's rally that will play out in the lives of our youth. If you're a culinary artist, would you consider contributing to our bake sale? All monies received will go toward that fund. Sign up on your way out at the welcome center.

Next, many of you know about the home in our community that was damaged by fire. Right now, this family needs to feel the full impact of God's domino effect in their lives, and we're lining up to make that happen as we partner with Habitat for Humanity to rebuild their home. Would you lean into God's call and sign up to take part in this project? You can learn more and sign up at the welcome center on your way out.

Lastly, God's domino effect is on full display in our church through the relationships that have developed over the generations here. On Tuesday night our women's ministry will gather for a time of food, faith, and fellow-

ship as they continue to live in close proximity and alignment with one another. If you're a lady (sorry guys), consider signing up at the welcome center on your way out. There are a few gals at the signup form that will answer any questions that you may have.

I'd invite you as you go into this week to be an extension of the movement that began with our Father, into the Son, into the disciples, throughout the church, and now moves into you. Go now and be a continuation of what God has set in motion. Amen.

Crafting the language around the theme packs a punch, ties it to the day's narrative, and takes the theoretical ideas presented in the sermon and turns them into practical action steps while the information is fresh. One church Jason coaches near Minneapolis, Minnesota, implemented this shift, and the pastor remarked, "Once we made this move, we went from no one signing up for anything, to people rushing to the sign-up forms after worship was over. We only have a fifteen-passenger van, and if you aren't on the list early, you have to drive yourself. It's made us a lot more missional." Of course, you'll likely still have external mission projects, which we'll explore later in this chapter that do not connect to worship, but don't miss the chance to make mission a part of the Sunday morning experience.

Reflection Questions:

What can you do to enhance the environment in the worship you offer?

How would you categorize the music you offer in worship and does it fit with how you categorize your worship?

How are you integrating creativity/theme throughout worship including the sermon?

What can you to do be more "action oriented" through worship?

Guest Readiness

The second key ingredient that should be included in your local dive recipe is that of hospitality, first impressions, and guest readiness. We have to have worship worth coming to, but we also have to be mindful that it's not automatic that people will come back if they aren't intentionally welcomed.

Think of it like visiting a new restaurant. If you walk in and it takes forever to get seated, or if the server is rude, if your drinks aren't refilled, or if the wrong food is brought out, you might decide never to return even if the food ends up being phenomenal. If the experience surrounding worship doesn't match up to the incredible preaching, inspiring music, and experiential worship, people won't come back. We have to earn second, third, and ongoing visits.

Guest readiness means being poised for newcomers. An important shift we need to make is to refer to new attendees as guests rather than visitors. Jason's friend Greg Atkinson, who is an author, consultant, and the founder of the First Impressions conference, says, "Visitors are unexpected. Guests are prepared for." He points out that when a visitor knocks on your door, you may not be ready in that moment to host them. You might have a sink full of dishes. The house may be cluttered. When you are expecting a guest, you tidy up. You put fresh linens on the bed. You make everything just right."

Whether you're starting something new, or revamping something old, be sure to consider how ready you are to receive guests.

From Transactional to Relational

Another important shift that we must make is from transactional thinking to relational thinking. There are many ways we approach first time guests in a transactional way. From handing them a printed piece (bulletin/program/worship folder) to handing them a coffee mug on the way out. These acts in and of themselves aren't bad, but our approach to them often is.

The act of greeting and gift giving is a transaction, but the conversation and connections we make around those acts are opportunities to form relationships with guests. The relationship begins before the visit. Our websites can be transactional in that we give people the times our worship meets, but no descriptions of what to expect. Or we use simple, one-word descriptors like "traditional" and "contemporary."

When you invite people to your local dive via your website, invite people relationally into your community by creating robust descriptions of the worship experiences you offer. Describe the music, the atmosphere, how they should dress, and anything else that might put them at ease and give them an indication of what they can expect. Show them pictures of your community and your space. Even your website's staff section is important for shifting from transactional to relational. A staff section is often a list of names, titles, and contact info. Instead, use this section to invite people into a relationship. To be more relational, you staff section should include these three items:

1. **Photo of each staff person** – Let them see who you are, get to know your face. These photos should be consistent from staff member to staff member. In other words, avoid using a black and white photo for one staff member, a color photo for another, a casual shot from a smartphone for another, and a professional photo for yet another. They should all look the same.
2. **A way to contact the person** – Include a phone number, but more importantly, an email address. Many people today are phone-averse and prefer to start conversations via text.
3. **Vision statement/bio** – Perhaps the most important item on the list is the inclusion of a vision statement/bio. This helps guests get to know your staff and understand what drives them. When a children's minister talks about their passion for raising up children in the way of Jesus, a greater impact and first impression will be made.

Guests will be drawn to your church when the relationships began prior to walking through the front door.

Another way to extend the relationship is to livestream your worship on social media. In the year prior to publishing this book, we've seen a dramatic increase in the number of newcomers who become worshipers at churches that broadcast their worship services to Facebook and other social media platforms. Walking into a church requires a higher level of vulnerability than watching in the comfort of one's home. Guests can check you out online prior to committing to the potential awkwardness of coming to your physical location.

Churches who are doing this well are even assigning online pastors to host chats, offer words of welcome to visitors, and more. Some even offer a guest gift online.

Avoiding Unspoken Rituals

Without meaning to, even when we're starting something new, we can unintentionally be insider focused. Practices develop almost immediately that have meaning for our community, but are confusing and even off-putting to first-time guests.

Sometimes the franchise recipe is too present in the local dive, meaning we continue rituals and practices that are part of the tradition. Other times, we do things without much consideration that the outsider might not understand what's happening. It's always a good idea to offer explanations of the weekly rituals we participate in.

Jason was recently secret worshiping at a wonderful church outside Denver, Colorado. The pastor and leaders are always tweaking the recipe and embrace the local dive mentality. Just as worship began, Jason was handed a basket from the person sitting behind him. Perplexed, Jason wondered what the purpose of the basket was. He wondered if they were taking offering, but it seemed too early to do so. Seeing Jason stare at the basket in confusion, a congregant leaned forward and whispered in Jason's ear that the basket was for prayer requests. Jason didn't have any paper or writing utensils, so he handed the basket to the person next to him. While all of this was taking place, the pastor was sharing announcements and opening words, which Jason completely missed as he was trying to make sense of what had just taken place. It was only moments later that he realized there were pieces of paper and pencils in the seat in front of him.

The ritual of taking up prayer requests in a basket isn't a bad thing. Doing so without orienting a newcomer to the practice is. Consider another successful church plant Jason secret worshiped at in the Chicago area, whose unspoken ritual was unsettling for Jason's introverted wife. After a time of welcome and offering, the pastor announced that they needed to find their "holy tear-er" for the moment. When those words were spoken, they were perceived as "holy terror." The pastor moved about the room looking at the people in the audience until she chose one and brought them forward to the front of the worship space. Any first-time visitor experiencing this would wish they could melt into their seat! Jason's wife sat watching nervously, hoping she would not be picked to be the holy tear-er—whatever that was!

Once chosen, the holy tear-er then tore off the perforated sections of the attendance cards and tossed them in a basket as a record of attendance that morning.

This ritual caused anxiety for Jason's wife and would likely have confused any guest in attendance. Had the ritual been preceded by an explanation — *"We have a little tradition that we do every week. We pick what we call the 'holy tear-er.' This person tears off our attendance cards and we celebrate all who are gathered. Now it's time to pick the holy tear-er."* — it would have made the moment less "insider."

TRANSFORMATION CHURCH, CHARLOTTE, NC

Even large, successful local dives can suffer from the insider language problem. In the fall of 2018, Jason was co-leading a weekend retreat and took a group of ministers to Transformation Church, a large church in the Charlotte area. Transformation Church is doing spectacular ministry. They do a wonderful job with guest readiness, and their worship is inspiring. Yet, there was a moment at the conclusion of worship that left Jason feeling like a complete outsider.

Pastor Derwin Grey offered some closing words, and then, without any explanation, pointed his fingers up in the air speaking a phrase, pointing left uttering another phrase, pointing right offering another phrase, and then spinning his hands and saying, "Transformers roll out." While all of this was taking place, the congregation joined in perfect unison, with the hand motions in perfect sync. The moment played out as a fun rally cry for the regulars, but for outsiders, it felt like a secret handshake.

Again, the ritual isn't bad. In fact, it's actually pretty cool. All that would need to be tweaked to make it something everyone could participate in is to tell people what's coming, show them the motions and display the words on the screen.

Watch Insider Language

Closely related to unspoken rituals is the use of insider language. Even a local dive can carry in language that makes no sense to a non-believer or new believer. The way we name things is important in the church. Rather than using archaic language to describe our spaces and practices like *narthex*, *sanctuary*, *bulletin*, *benediction*, and so on, we might consider language that is more guest friendly. *Welcome center*, *auditorium*, *program*, and *blessing* all have more resonance for the outsider.

CAUTION: ENTERING NARTHEX

Narthex, which sounds a lot like the cow disease *anthrax*, sounds like a room you need a hazmat suit to enter: not very welcoming. The word *sanctuary* brings images of birds and nature preserves to mind. The only time you hear the word *bulletin* outside church is when the police are searching for someone. And *benediction* reminds us of the man who betrayed the Continental Army before defecting to the British.

These words have meaning to those of us who acquired a taste for them, but for the outsider they can be intimidating. We don't have to throw them out entirely, but we should intentionally build bridges to them if we want outsiders to understand their value and meaning.

Years ago, Jason was conducting a secret worshiper consultation in Las Vegas, Nevada, a place where there are often guests at worship. The pastor had created a second worship experience with a more contemporary flare and asked Jason to share observations about what might be hard for an outsider or new believer to comprehend.

Without giving it much thought, the pastor said during the sermon, "You all know about the power of the Holy Eucharist, right?" Jason observed a woman in the row in front of him say to her young daughter, "Nope." The daughter innocently replied, "You've never heard of the Holy Uterus?" Jason nearly fell out of his seat. At the conclusion of worship, Jason shared with the pastor what he had heard. He said it felt as though he was receiving an anatomy lesson. The pastor responded, "Maybe I should have said 'Holy Communion' instead." Jason agreed.

But then, even *communion* is a word that must be explained. We have to be mindful that this ritual is something we've learned over time. Avoid doing the short version of communion saying, "Let us eat this flesh and drink this blood." Some guests might start looking for the door.

Watching our language is important when using ancient church language, but we must also be considerate of outsiders with words that are only connected to our communities. The United Methodist Church has a long-established ministry often referred to by its acronym, UMW. Any good

United Methodist can tell you in an instant that those letters stand for the United Methodist Women's group. At a recent seminar, a participant shared that growing up in Pennsylvania, those letters always stood for the United Mine Workers. When the participant first joined a Methodist Church, she kept wondering why there were such fervent supports of the miners' union. Months later, she learned what the acronym meant to Methodists.

Another church Jason consulted with in Texas had a sign hanging outside the door of its classroom that read, "Co-Workers." Jason took that to mean that it was the break room or a place for employees of the church to gather. It might as well have read "Employees Only." After worship, Jason asked about the sign, and the staff told him that was their adult Sunday school class. Jason remarked that he would never have gone into that classroom because he didn't work here and had no understanding of the language.

Parentheses can serve us well when it comes to signage. The sign could read "Adult Sunday School," and in parentheses, "Co-Workers." The sign above the sanctuary door can read "Auditorium," and in parentheses say "Sanctuary."

Reduce "Forced Interaction"

For a new guest, attending a new place of worship can feel like showing up at someone else's family reunion. Our guests don't yet love us and aren't even sure that they want to return. The truth is, we often ask too much of our first-time guests in worship.

One of the most unexpectedly reviled practices in the church is greeting time. In some circles this might be called "passing the peace," in others it might be the meet- 'n'-greet, and in others it's just the welcome time.

According to writer Thom Rainer, this is the number one reason visitors don't return to church. In his blog article, "Top Ten Ways Churches Drive Away First-Time Guests," Rainer reports that most respondents to a Twitter poll he conducted over a period of months chose this as the reason they don't want to return.[114] Reading through the comments on this post further paints the picture that the practice makes most folks uncomfortable.

This certainly lines up with our experience as well. For about ten years, Jason has been conducting seminars on Guest Readiness. At one point in the day, Jason conducts an anonymous poll (all eyes closed with votes cast by raising a hand) with participants answering first who enjoys this practice. He then asks how many dislike it and wish that it would go away. The results are remarkably consistent. Usually about 20-30% like it and 70-80% dislike it. These are leaders in the area of hospitality. It's their job to consider these things.

Why is this forced interaction so potentially damaging for our local dives? Because it doesn't give people an opportunity to ease into our communities. Think about it. If you have a significant other in your life, your relationship was a progression. First it was talking with one another. Maybe it progressed to a date. Then holding hands, possibly a kiss on

---

[114] www.TomRainer.com. "Top Ten Ways Churches Drive Away First-Time Guests." Accessed December 9, 2019.

the cheek, and so on. When guests come into our churches, we give them no choice but to shake our hands, or even hug us, before they have any connection to our community.

Outside of the church, it is rare to hold hands with, hug, or even shake the hand of a perfect stranger. Yet some of us do this every week in worship. Jason is an extrovert. This practice isn't a problem for him. But his wife is an introvert and would rather arrive at worship ten minutes late than have to participate in this practice. Whether you hate it or love it, here are four people you need to consider when developing guest readiness practices for your local dive, and three solutions for allowing it to happen in a guest-friendly way.

1. **Introverts** – Believe it or not, extroverts, there are people who find it painful to have to have conversation on the spot with strangers. It takes energy and effort, and it often drains them. Beginning worship with a forced greeting time can be excruciating for introverts.

2. **People averse to touch** – There are people who have a history of negative touch in their lives. For example, being touched can be uncomfortable for those with a history of sexual abuse. Many of us have congregants who refuse a handshake and will go for a hug each and every time.

There are also those among us who have sensory issues that make touch uncomfortable. Jason's son Ethan has Sensory Processing Disorder. Touch can be uncomfortable for him. When Jason places his hands on Ethan's shoulders when he's at the table doing homework, Ethan often squirms out of it saying, "Ugh, stop dad. That makes me uncomfortable."

Jason recently visited a church and went to shake the hand of a young man, only to be warned by the person standing next to him that the man was autistic and that touch was difficult for him. He tends to have a loud and visceral reaction it.

3. **Germaphobes** – There are people who don't like to shake hands or embrace because they're afraid to get sick, especially during cold and flu season.

   Comedian and gameshow host Howie Mandel suffers from a condition that makes it nearly impossible for him to touch others around him. He typically offers fist bumps, and steers clear of shaking hands. In one controversial episode of the hit TV show America's Got Talent, Howie was hypnotized into believing he was wearing invisible gloves that would allow him to shake hands with those around him.[115] When the hypnotism was over, and he reviewed the tapes, he was distraught by what had taken place. He says he would not have participated if he'd known what was going to happen. If someone like Howie walks into your church, and you begin worship with a moment of forced greeting time, how would that set him up for failure or success in your community?

4. **People with compromised immune systems** – At two different seminars, Jason was recently told that the greeting time was preventing church members from attending church.

   At one church, the pastor told Jason that he had a member of his church who was undergoing chemotherapy and that he was told not to make physical contact with others and to avoid handshakes and hugs. This pastor was lamenting that his congregation was so married to this practice that they did so disregarding concern for this member, who had to stay home.

---

[115] Hines, Renee. TODAY. Today.com. "Pop culture: Howie Mandel Says AGT Hypnotism Act Didn't Cure Him." https://www.today.com/popculture/howie-mandel-says-agt-hypnotism-act-didnt-cure-him-t23106. Accessed December 18, 2019.

The other shared that an elderly member of the congregation had an autoimmune disease that made her susceptible to contracting illnesses through physical contact, which meant she more or less had to stay home. Despite the pastor's best efforts, the congregation refused to give up the practice.

So, do all these types of people coming to our churches as guests mean we have to ban greeting time? No. It's not all bad, but for many it is off-putting.

Here are three ways to make it work for the groups mentioned here:

1. **Let them bow out** – During greeting time, consider giving people an opportunity to bow their heads in silent prayer. Give instructions to clue both them and the rest of the congregation in to this opportunity to bow out: "Friends, now is the time in worship when we greet one another. If you're new with us, or that would be uncomfortable for you today, we'd invite you to bow your head in silent prayer right there in your seat. We'll honor your posture, as we greet one another, then we'll invite everyone to stand and sing." This eliminates the forced part of the practice and allows people to join in as they feel comfortable doing so.

2. **Impose Limits** – At many churches, the greeting time goes on way too long. For visitors, this can be excruciating. What often happens is that a guest is greeted by one or two people, and then they stand there awkwardly when the rest of the room continues the practice for another four or five minutes.

   We've been to churches where people in the front row go all the way to the back row and vice-versa. We've seen congregants go from the balcony or the stage to the first floor to greet one another, losing valuable time in the service. We've even witnessed worship where worship doesn't re-start until every single person greets every single other person.

Imposing limits eliminates the awkwardness of that time for the people in the four categories mentioned earlier. It reins-in control of the service, and it can create more meaningful exchanges between people.

So, what is a limit? Limits can be time based: "You have ninety seconds to shake as many hands as you can." They can be location based: "Every other row, starting with the front, turn around and greet the people behind you." Or they can be based on other ideas, like: "Find one person to greet who is wearing the same color shoes as you are." Anything to keep the period brief and move on to the rest of worship.

3. **Move it to the end** – The pastor who Jason coached in Las Vegas, Pastor Michael Patzloff, offered a helpful solution for reclaiming this time in guest-friendly ways. His practice was to move it to the end of the service. He would announce:

   In a moment we're going to do something that we call "passing the peace." That basically means that we're going to greet each other in the name of Christ and offer words of peace to one another. For some of you that may feel uncomfortable and we understand that. Before we do that, I'm going to offer something we call the benediction. This is basically a blessing that will send you forth from this place out into the week.

   If passing the peace would be uncomfortable, you are welcome to slip out during the benediction. We won't judge you. And if you love passing the peace, we'd invite you to hang for our fellowship hour where we'll pass the peace around coffee and donuts. Let me now offer the benediction. Friends as you go into this week ....

From there he'd finish the benediction and people would slip out.

Pastor Michael said that he noticed that newcomers might slip out on their first few visits, but after a while they started to hang around. After they got comfortable with that, they might start attending the fellowship hour. What Michael discovered was that if we ease people into community, they are much more likely to organically be a part of it than they might be if we try to force them into it on day one.

One final thought to consider about greeting time. It's worth noting that people tend to greet one another prior to worship starting. People also tend to mingle and greet one another when worship is over. It's worth exploring whether a dedicated time within service is needed at all.

Another aspect of forced interaction that we should ask is, "Does this past the cringe test?" or, another way to say it is, "Does this past the neighbor test?" When you consider bringing your most secular neighbor to church, what moments are taking place that cause you to cringe? Make no mistake about it, we are not talking about compromising the gospel. We're talking about making it accessible to others in our rituals and practices.

Be careful about how vulnerable you ask people to be with one another in worship. Forced interactions like saying, "Turn to your neighbor and say..." can put guests and unchurched people (or even your regular attenders) into uncomfortable situations.

Jason recently attended a worship service, and the worship director said, "Turn to your neighbor and say, 'We serve an awesome God.'" For Jason, this is high on the cringe factor scale. Had he chosen to bring his secular neighbor to church, his neighbor faces a no-win scenario. The neighbor either has to turn to Jason, his actual neighbor, or to the stranger sitting on the other side of him, and awkwardly say, "We serve an awesome God." This person could very well not believe in God. The last thing he wants to say is that he serves an awesome God. His other choice is to sit and not participate when the people on either side of him are participating, making him stand out in a negative way.

Vulnerability is the key here. It doesn't hurt to turn to your neighbor and tell him/her your favorite food, for example. If that factors into your sermon, it's a perfectly acceptable ask. But asking people to turn to their neighbor and tell them your biggest temptation is asking guests to be too vulnerable.

Create Entry Points

The final component of guest readiness to consider is creating entry points for first-time guests. Creating opportunities for them to engage is extremely valuable. Many churches offer a first-time visitor gift. This can be a meaningful practice, but it can also be a waste of resources if not done well. For instance, if your visitor gift is a one-color (usually white), ceramic coffee mug sporting a one-color logo, it is very likely to end up in the trash. People can sniff out the fact that you ordered the cheapest mug you could find, and it's unlikely that this mug is going to become anyone's favorite after one time with you. In fact, at a recent Guest Readiness seminar, a woman told Jason she had been to her local Goodwill and noticed a shelf full of coffee mugs emblazoned with different church's logos. Most of us have

VISITOR GIFT OPTIONS

a cabinet full of coffee mugs, but we rotate through the same two or three favorites.

So, if this is what you're offering, stop! Instead, consider investing in nicer thermal coffee mugs that keep coffee warm and cold drinks cold. Print your logo on it as a reminder to guests that you exist. A thermal coffee mug is something people might actually take back and forth to work with them every day. It doesn't hurt to have your church's logos on them. Most of us have a cabinet already too full of coffee mugs. We tend to rotate through the same two or three favorites over and over, and they're not usually "plain Jane."

You might also consider adding a five-dollar gift card for a cup of coffee from a local coffee house so they can fill their cup on you. Include a note that says something like, "We want your lives to be filled with the Spirit and your next cup of coffee to be filled on us. Your friends at Local Dive Church."

Not everyone drinks coffee, so you might offer a higher quality sports water bottle with your church's logo. Again, don't go cheap here with the razor thin plastic water bottle. Invest in something people are likely to keep.

Another option is to donate a few dollars in the name of the guest to a local charity. Evidence suggests that millennials see logo-ed swag as a waste when the money could be used to help people in need.

REAL LIFE CHURCH, MOSCOW, ID

Jason observed an inspirational way to do this. The church had four plexiglass boxes built with the names of four charities affixed to them. Guests could choose which one they wanted the donation being made in their name to go to. In each of the boxes was a collection of colored ping-pong balls. Each time a guest chose a charity, a ball was dropped into the box. This was an excellent way to show how many new guests were coming to church, which charities were receiving the most attention, and for the guests, a way to see that their visit contributed to a mission.

You could do one, two, or all of these options, but don't think of them as a transaction. Think about them as a way of connecting in meaningful ways with your guests. The conversation you have with them when they come to retrieve their gift is as important as, if not more important than, what you're giving them to take home.

Offering options is a great way to get people to turn in those first-time guest cards. Very few of us are ready to give our personal information to people we don't know. Have you ever been on the Internet, clicked on a link to read an article, only to discover that you had to enter your email address to continue? For most of us, our next move is to close the window. The same mentality is true at church. We don't want to get spammed by a website, nor do we want to be spammed or harassed by a church we might visit again.

So why not show on the screen the first-time guest gifts that are available, tell them to check a box on the first-time guest card to indicate the one they want, and invite them to the welcome center to pick up their gift? They're more likely to share their info if you have a great take-home for them.

Other entry points might include a monthly "pizza or dessert with the pastor" when new people can have a light lunch and get to know the staff. One large church offers "The 10 Minute Party" after worship. Guests are invited there after worship to connect, have a cupcake, and learn more about the church. Considering the guest experience at your church might just be the secret sauce that makes all the difference.

Reflection Questions:

What are some ways you can move from transactional to relational in welcoming guests?

Are there unspoken rituals in your service that need to be eliminated or better explained?

How can you rethink forced interaction in your worship?

Community Building

Community has become a buzzword in Christian culture. It's often talked about and sought after in the church, but rarely with any practical suggestions. In many ways, community is caught before it's taught. When someone experiences community, they are in essence experiencing hospitality. To create community and a culture of hospitality in a church that is struggling takes practice, training, and repetition. In a culture where we're more connected than ever before, but also where many feel more lonely than ever before, community and relationship building matters more than ever before.

In many of the places Roz has pastored, he's been able to create this culture by engaging with people post-service. If a few of his leaders see people who are new, they often invite them to go to lunch with a group from the church. It's not hard or intrusive, especially if a new guest is alone. In different towns where Roz has pastored, he has kept a rotating list of restaurants so that hospitality leaders knew where to invite folks, give directions, and offer to sit with them. It's a small gesture that goes a long way. The role of being a hospitality leader is not for everyone. It's for your extroverted folks who love meeting and talking to new people. These team members shouldn't be engaged in post-service tasks like counting the offering or putting away supplies, but rather on the front lines identifying new guests.

Some examples of community building that can be done without breaking the bank are events like concerts in local parks, outdoor movies, coffee hour where you can partner with a local coffee shop to pay for people's coffee, and Kona Ice Truck day. People are more likely to accept an invitation to a community event than to a worship service for the first time. Community building events encourage connections between regular attenders and new guests, and also serve as a front door to the church for the community. These events don't take a lot of work. They involve making connections in the community to find space to hold concerts and movie nights (Parks and Rec can be a great partner), Kona Ice is inexpensive and fun to do on a hot summer day, and a coffee hour can be the right atmosphere to meet new people who are curious about why a church would buy their coffee. These events are tools to create engagement and conversation. There are many other ideas local churches can come up with as they scan their context and look for partnerships.

Reflection Questions:

What are some natural community building partnerships you can form?

What percentage of time are you spending in the community versus inside the church?

Discipleship pathway

Real discipleship doesn't happen in rows on Sunday morning. It happens in circles of people doing life together wrestling though challenging questions and engaged in scripture.

As people integrate into your local dive, they're naturally going to want to know what is next. Discipleship is a process. It doesn't happen automatically. How do people plug in to your community? It will depend on the structure you create, and whether you are part of an existing church or a multi-site. You will have to make the decision at the outset about whether the pathways to discipleship will be uniform or autonomous. If the existing ministry has a defined structure for classes and small groups, will the new thing follow that structure as well? If a curriculum is used, will it be used in both settings?

There are two primary strategies that discipleship pathways may be built. They can be class driven or small group driven. Of course, you'd ideally have both options present, but when you're building new things, it's hard to do everything at once. One is not better than the other. They both have value and context will determine the best fit.

Small Groups

Small groups are the way to go if people like to meet in homes. If you don't have a dedicated space, being small group driven may be dictated by your resources. Jesus spent the majority of His ministry investing in a small group of twelve disciples. Discipleship happens in small groups in ways that it doesn't happen in a larger setting. People tend to go deeper in their relationships and in their faith when gathered in smaller groups where safe space can be established.

Small groups should be intimate, easy to join, and have some degree of structure to be successful. They should also be organized in such a way that they are congruent with the church's vision and purpose. There is a plethora of ways that small groups can be organized. And we won't go into a deep dive here. There are plenty of books on that topic.

Class-Driven

Class-driven studies are larger and typically meet in the confines of a church building. While relationship building can happen in these settings, the relationships tend to be less intimate.

A class-driven discipleship pathway may use pre-produced materials such as Alpha, Financial Peace University, Disciple Bible Study, and the like. Some churches are seeing success with asynchronous studies offered online in social media settings such as Facebook.

Class-driven studies might also include original curriculum written in conjunction with series that are taking place at the church. In many churches, worship and discipleship are like ships passing in the night. They are often disconnected and have no real relationship with one another. Worship series with simultaneous classes attached give us an opportunity to dig deeper into the concepts being explored.

For instance, the *Set in Motion* series we've referenced might include a multiple week class, learning about one's spiritual gifts, then putting them into action in the world. This exploration would invite participants to see how we can continue to build on God's domino rally in the world by "remaining in His love."

With a strategy chosen, leaders will need to be trained according to context as well. Necessary skills differ for table leaders and small group leaders who welcome people into their homes. The ultimate goal is to produce fruitful discipleship of Jesus Christ.

At various churches Roz has pastored, he has initiated core discipleship pathways such as Alpha, Financial Peace University, and a spiritual gifts-based class. Roz has found that small groups tend to happen organically. Whatever the case, it's important that everyone understands what it means to take the next steps of their spiritual journey in your church.

Reflection Questions:

Are you a class-driven or small groups driven ministry?

How are you pouring into leaders?

What are your core classes?

Mission

The final critical component is to reach your local context is missions. We don't experience the fullness of our faith until we put it into action. Creating action-oriented churches keeps people coming back because parishioners live both in the theory and practice of being a disciple of Jesus Christ.

We've shared how worship can be the front door into discipleship. None of these essential ingredients stand alone. They all overlap, and mission is no different. The local church should not be siloed. Chances are, there are other organizations and nonprofits already working for the common good in your community.

There is no need to re-invent the wheel or become an expert in a specific type of ministry that already exists. When starting a new thing, it is easy to spread yourself too thin. If there are food pantries in your area, maybe you make an effort to support them. If there's a free store, you could collect items to stock it. How can you partner with organizations doing these kinds of ministries?

For example, during the Memorial Day tornadoes of 2019 in Dayton, Ohio, Roz's church collaborated with other churches in cleanup efforts, started a letter-writing campaign to local students who were starting school late, and initiated a school supply drive for students who were affected by the devastation of nineteen tornadoes. Not only did the efforts spur on Mosaic Church, but other churches, organizations, and individuals as well.

Remember also that there are many entry points into our faith communities. Some people will come out to help in disaster recovery or feeding the hungry who have no connection to the church or faith. Being active in mission gives us another avenue to make meaningful relationships with people all around us.

Whatever you decide to do as a local congregation to meet the needs of your community, the call is to cook up a meal that is favorable to your context. The recipe and flavor will vary, but the effort in the kitchen should be maximized to reach as many hungry people as possible.

Reflection Questions:

How are you doing local missions?

Are there ministries or organizations in your community you can partner with?

CHAPTER 8

TO GO BOX

NEXT STEPS

Whether dining at a franchise or local dive, sometimes the meal is so good, and you're so full, you simply can't eat it all in one sitting. When you love the food enough to take it home, you ask the waiter for a "to go" box.

This last section is really the same idea. There are so many ideas to chew on in this book that it could become very overwhelming to try and implement everything right away.

It might also be tempting to look at one of the many recipes we've shared and try and copy it for your own setting. Please don't do that.

In 1985, when the very first pair of Nike Air Jordan's were released, they were the envy of sneakerheads everywhere. That year, when Jason's mom took him back to school shopping, they were at the top of his wish list.

Jason came from a middle-class family, and the budget for apparel was fairly modest. Still, when his mother took him to the shoe store, he had his eyes set on those black, red, and white Jordan's.

Surprisingly, when Jason found a pair at the shoe store, he discovered that they were within the budget allotted by his parents for shoes. He tried them on, took them to the counter, and his mother made the purchase.

Giddy, that night he dreamed of what the next day at school would be like. He couldn't wait to show off his new shoes. There were only two major problems. First, they hadn't been shopping at Footlocker or The Finish Line that day. They had stopped by the local Payless Shoes store.

The second problem was that the shoes Jason took home were red, black, and white, and the pattern was nearly identical. Only missing from the shoes were the famous Nike swoosh and the words "Air Jordan." Jason had taken home a bootleg/knockoff version of the popular shoe.

BOOTLEG VERSION

The kids were quick to point this reality out to him on the next day. Thankfully, Payless allowed Jason to return the shoes that evening, but an important lesson was learned. Don't buy the bootleg version of the popular thing someone else is doing.

We've exposed you to many highly successful franchises and local dives in this book. Each and every one had to figure out a recipe that worked for them. If you lift wholesale what someone else is doing, you may find yourself like Jason did on the first day of school with a recipe destined to fail.

As you think about your to go box, we want to offer you a few final thoughts.

1. What's One Thing?

There are – we hope – many things you've read in these pages that you'd like to implement right away. Resist the temptation to do all of them right away. Figure out what the one big thing you should do first is and live into that. Surround it with your attention and resources. Work it out. Make it happen. Then start thinking about the next big thing.

If you try to do everything at once, you can crash and burn pretty quickly – especially if you're trying to revitalize something old. People can only take so much change at once.

2. Develop a Purpose/Vision Statement

You can't know everything that lies ahead, but you can (with a lot of intentional work), create a picture worth living in to. Writing a vision statement that captures the "why" of what you're doing is of the utmost importance. The "what" you're doing is different than the "why" you're doing it. As comedian Michael Jr. says, "When you know your 'why,' your 'what' becomes more impactful because you're walking towards or in your purpose." [116]

You must also consider the "who" you're trying to reach. As mentioned earlier, determining your target audience is key to the strategies you create. Lastly, looking back on that covenant agreement and the Franchise to Local Dive Continuum is a great way to establish shared expectations.

3. Begin Your Plan

Procrastination can be such a deterrent to fulfilling your call to start something new. It is so easy to wait until you have every single question answered, every detail debated and decided, and every other concern triple checked. We certainly encourage you to do a lot of work up front to think about what recipe you're going to create before you try to cook it, but don't let trying to perfect it stop you from actually starting.

Do the work, establish the teams, find the space, but be firm on when you're going to start. Opening day has to come at some point, and it's likely not going to be perfect the first time no matter what you do.

4. Iterate

There is freedom to keep tweaking the recipe, so iterate and keep trying new things after you've launched. It doesn't have to be perfect on day one. Ideally, it should look different on day one hundred than it does on day one. Keep the spirit of "the test kitchen" alive at all costs.

---

[116] Michael Jr. "Know Your Why." https://www.youtube.com/watch?v=1ytFB8Trk-To&t=6s. Accessed December 18, 2019.

Be careful to avoid working in a template. Just because something works, doesn't mean that you have to do it over and over again. You'll eventually wear it out.

Clay Mathile, founder of the Iams Company and Dayton, Ohio native once said, "The only difference between a rut and a groove is how long you've been in it." [117]

Those powerful words remind us that we have to always keep experimenting and iterating our recipe. Strive to keep it fresh. Make something special. Keep that food truck mentality alive. If we forget these things, it's inevitable that in time we'll create the same culture of exclusivity that shut the people of Ezra's day out from the good news.

Friends, the world we live in is hungry. They need to be invited to taste and see that the Lord is good. Jesus tells us that we are the salt of the earth. Go out there and make things spicy. Cook up something that will change the world!

Let's keep the conversation going. We've taken the show on the road and have interviewed many of the planters in the book live on camera for what we're calling *Franchise to Local Dive Road Show.* Visit:

www.franchise2dive.com

to view the interviews, learn about seminars based on the book and more.

[117] Biz e-mom. "Between a Rut and a Groove?" https://bizemom.wordpress.com/2011/02/05/between-a-rut-and-a-groove/?fbclid=IwAR2IM1AgM17A0b8y-i3jIzQe3ckGX3_qLq2BaR8AoeuIkAeJEGsNpDAYHoE. Accessed December 18, 2019.

Other Books

from Market Square

marketsquarebooks.com

Other Books

from Market Square

marketsquarebooks.com

Wesleyan Grace Theology

Dr. Donald Haynes

From Heaven to Earth Advent Study

Wil Cantrell & Paul Seay

Church Ecology

Creating a Leadership Pathway for your Church

Ken Willard & Kelly Brown

The Methodist Story Volume I ▪ 1703-1791

Dr. Donald Haynes

Grow Your Faith

with these books from Market Square

marketsquarebooks.com

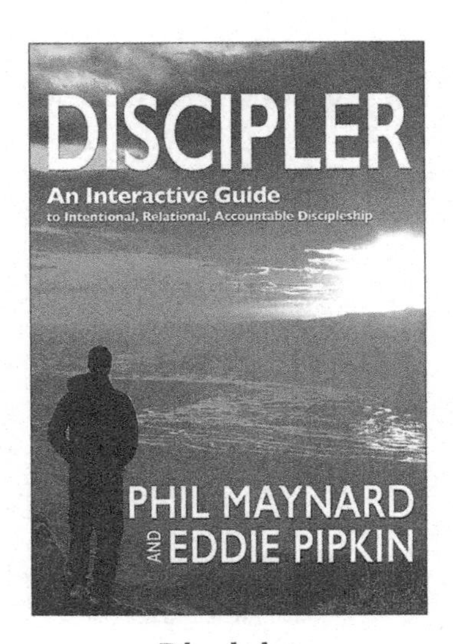

Discipler

Phil Maynard & Eddie Pipkin

Hear It, See It, Risk It

Steve Cordle

A Christian Teenager's
Guide to Surviving High School

Ashley Conner

Understanding Your Call
11 Biblical Figures Understand Their Calls from God

by 10 United Methodist Leaders

Latest Titles

from Market Square Books

marketsquarebooks.com

Dream Like Jesus
Bring the Impossible to Life
Rebekah Simon-Peter

Strategy Matters
Your Roadmap to an Effective Ministry Planning Retreat
Kay Kotan & Ken Willard

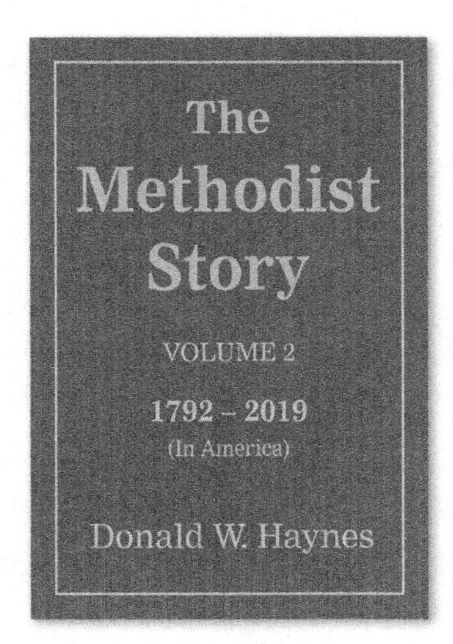

The Methodist Story
Volume 2 ▪ 1792-2019
Dr. Donald W. Haynes

Launching Leaders
Leadership Development
Kay Kotan and Phil Schroeder

Made in the USA
Monee, IL
06 April 2020

24682436R00138